ADVANCE PRAISE FOR *WHAT KIND OF CITIZEN?*

"Westheimer has written a necessary and brilliant book . . . one of the best in the last decade to take on what it means to reclaim ~~ the service of democratic values and ·~ akes clear that schools are at the heart ping young people who can create a fu *What Kind of Citizen?* is a manifesto for a racy that matters, and for a notion of ju

—Henr, ..., Global Television Network Chair in Communication Studies, McMaster University

"What does it mean to be a democratic citizen? And what kind of education produces one? For the past two decades, Joel Westheimer has been one of North America's most knowledgeable and able guides to these critical issues. Along the way, he has forced us to reconsider the larger goals and purposes of our public schools. His book will provide an invaluable roadmap for anyone who asks the big questions."

—Jonathan Zimmerman, professor of education and history, New York University

"Providing practicing educators with a goldmine of information and examples, this book indicates, once again, that Westheimer is one of the most prolific, original, and visionary scholars doing citizenship education work and research."

—James A. Banks, Kerry and Linda Killinger Endowed Chair in Diversity Studies and Director, Center for Multicultural Education, University of Washington

"Joel Westheimer argues persuasively that the current emphasis on standardization in the schools not only diminishes teacher professionalism, but conflicts with citizenship education."

—Diane Ravitch, Professor of Education at New York University, historian of education, author of *Reign of Error*

"Among the many casualties of a preoccupation with rigor and accountability is the prospect of education for meaningful democratic citizenship. In this refreshingly accessible book, Westheimer not only makes that point but explains the importance of helping students to think critically and question tradition. He issues a welcome invitation to connect our conception of the ideal school to its impact on our broader society."

—Alfie Kohn, author of *Feel-Bad Education* and *The Myth of the Spoiled Child*

"With *What Kind of Citizen?* Westheimer distinguishes himself as a leading thinker and activist in the radical tradition of W.E.B. DuBois, John Dewey, bell hooks, and Fanny Coppin."

—William Ayers,
School Reform Activist and author of *Teaching the Taboo: Courage and Imagination in the Classroom, Second Edition*

"This brilliant little book calls for personal and collective responsibility among our students that doesn't amount to just volunteering on projects, but that attempts to remedy areas of unfairness and injustice. Westheimer's book makes the case for civic and critical engagement of our students rather than a standardized curriculum. This book is compelling, very accessible, full of inspiring examples and sometimes even funny."

—Andy Hargreaves,
Thomas More Brennan Chair in Education, Boston College

"In this highly readable, persuasive book, Joel Westheimer reminds us that, in our zeal for higher test scores, we seem to have forgotten the highest aim of education—to produce better people, more thoughtful citizens."

—Nel Noddings,
Lee Jacks Professor of Education Emerita, Stanford University

"In this practical, personal, and hopeful work, Joel Westheimer asks us to imagine the kind of people we want to be—and how schools can help us become those people. *What Kind of Citizen?* cracks open the pleasing but often myopic lingo of citizenship education. Readers are left with an alternative vision of schooling that speaks directly to today's social and environmental crises—and to young people's hunger for a meaningful life."

—Bill Bigelow, Curriculum Editor, Rethinking Schools

"Westheimer is practitioner, critic, and visionary. This book is a wake-up call to rethink the real purpose of education. This is a must read for teachers, students, parents and anyone interested in finding deeper meaning for educating our children."

—Pasi Sahlberg, author of *Finnish Lessons 2.0: What Can the World Learn from Educational Change in Finland?*

"Dr. Westheimer, in this timely and important book, refocuses the attention of policymakers on providing students with learning experiences that equip them for engaged citizenship and ensuring that teachers have the professional autonomy and trust to do that work."

—Diane Woloschuk,
President, Canadian Teachers' Federation

What Kind of Citizen?

Educating Our Children for the Common Good

Joel Westheimer

TEACHERS COLLEGE PRESS
TEACHERS COLLEGE | COLUMBIA UNIVERSITY
NEW YORK AND LONDON

Published by Teachers College Press, 1234 Amsterdam Avenue, New York, NY 10027

Copyright © 2015 by Teachers College, Columbia University

An excerpt from Holly Near's "Great Peace March" (on Singer in the Storm, 1990) is reprinted in Chapter 10 by permission of HollyNear.com

Library of Congress Cataloging-in-Publication Data is available at loc.gov

ISBN 978-0-8077-5635-5 (paper)
ISBN 978-0-8077-7369-7 (ebook)

Printed on acid-free paper
Manufactured in the United States of America

22 21 20 19 18 17 16 15   8 7 6 5 4 3 2 1

Contents

Introduction

The only time I remember my mother speaking directly, and with great sadness, about leaving Germany on a *kindertransport* at the age of 10, was when I was back in Frankfurt with her some 40 years after it happened. I was 19 or 20 years old. We were waiting for a train together in the Frankfurt *Hauptbahnhof* (central station). I saw her look at a platform adjacent to the one where we were standing, and she said, "That's where I waved goodbye to my mother and grandmother—it looks exactly the same." And, indeed, it did. From both photographs and history books, I knew that although the allied bombing of Frankfurt destroyed much of the city, the central train station suffered only broken windows and minor damage. Only the advertising looked different. My mother remembers smiling while she waved goodbye so that her mother would not cry. She also remembers giving her favorite doll to the girl seated opposite her who was disconsolate. They were 2 of the 100 girls and boys on the train headed to relative safety in Switzerland. It was the last time my mother would see her family.

Just as I was beginning to write this book, I was asked to write a short intellectual autobiography exploring how my life experiences influenced the scholarly work I chose to pursue. It was a challenging task. Anyone who has attempted to put life experiences onto paper (or screen) knows that it too easily strips those experiences of their vitality and meaning. Yet pen and paper (keyboard and screen) are the tools of my trade. They are imperfect tools, but they are the tools I have. And so I opened the autobiography with my recollections of that moment on the train platform in Frankfurt, not because it was the first experience, chronologically speaking, that shaped my scholarly endeavors, or even the most important one. I started there because, although my parents—both German Jewish refugees—spoke relatively little about their experiences during World War II, I suspect that the intellectual and emotional lineage I inherited was shaped by the profound injustices that informed their childhoods.

> This book asks you to imagine the kind of society you would like to live in and shows how schools might best be used to make that vision a reality.

This book asks you to imagine the kind of society you would like to live in and shows how schools might best be used to make that vision a reality. Although the topic is highly political (school reform always is), it is also deeply personal. It has been said that we don't choose areas of intellectual inquiry, but rather, they choose us. I'm willing to bet my work in education, citizenship, and democratic community is the aboveground product of scholarly concerns with deeper roots. For as long as I can remember, I have been interested in the ways people treat one another, learn from one another, and live together in communities, local, national, and global—in short, how people see themselves as citizens. Education has always provoked my deepest passions, not because of the debates about passing fads and strategies (phonics versus whole language, new math versus old math, small classes versus big classes), but rather because choices about how we teach our children are choices about the kind of society we believe in and the kind of people we hope will emerge from our schoolhouse doors. Will they be concerned only with their own individual success and ambitions without regard to the welfare of others? Will they learn how to develop convictions and stand up for those convictions if and when it becomes necessary to do so?

Since you're reading this, you're probably interested in what schools might teach young people about being a citizen—a member of society—and what that society could look like if schools got it right. When we think about what schools should teach and how they should teach it, we quickly become tangled in the long and complex history of school reform and the contested role of education in democratic societies. In other words, "What kind of citizen?" is neither just an "academic" question (interesting in theory, but of little consequence to real life) nor an abstract one. It's a real question with real consequences for the kind of society we hope to create.

I've worked in many different educational environments in the United States, Canada, and abroad, as a teacher, camp director, youth organizer, and professor of education. Wherever I've been involved, I've become increasingly convinced of the importance of attending to the ways in which the educational program and its staff and participants think about civic communities and the people (or citizens) that comprise them. What kind of citizens does this institution hope its participants will become? When I ask teachers, students, parents, principals, and even school superintendents to tell me about their ideal school, the places they imagine are always vastly different from the images of schools conveyed by, for example, the standardized-testing industry, or politicians and school reformers focused on international "competitiveness." Much of the research I will tell you about in this book, placed in its broadest context, focuses on why this discrepancy is the case and what we can do about it. Teaching about citizenship is not solely the purview of social studies or a civics education class. The entire school is party to the enterprise.

What does an ideal school look like in your mind? What lessons are being conveyed? How are children and teachers interacting? What kinds of responsibilities are students being asked to take on? What vision of the "good" society is this school asking students to imagine? Are they learning to think about the kind of society *they* want to live in? Are they learning the skills and habits they would need to help bring that society into being? Are they learning to recognize injustice and work with others in their communities to diminish it? These are the questions that are considered in the chapters that follow.

I prefer to think about schools, not as vehicles for the transmission of knowledge (though they are that too), but as places where children learn about the society in which they are growing up, how they might engage in productive ways, and how they can fight for change when change is warranted.

Schools have always taught lessons in citizenship, moral values, good behavior, and "character." Even before there was formal schooling, informal education was replete with these kinds of goals. Contemporary schools inevitably teach these lessons as well. For example, schools teach children to follow rules, and to be sure, sometimes following the rules is necessary. But does being a "good" citizen ever require questioning those rules? What is the proper balance between rule following and thinking about the origins and purpose of those rules? We can imagine classrooms that aspire to that balance. But just because schools teach children about citizenship and character, doesn't mean they always do it well or even toward admirable aims. In fact, schools and other youth organizations have been enlisted in some of the worst forms of citizenship indoctrination as well. Counted among the many examples of organized "citizenship" education are the hateful lessons learned by members of the Hitler Youth brigades who were the same age as my mother when she boarded the train to Switzerland.

My goal in writing this book is not to convince you that schools should teach citizenship—because that is a given. I write this book because, knowing that schools are always instruments of citizenship education, it seems vitally important that educators, policymakers, and parents—anyone who cares about education and society—ask not whether schools should teach citizenship but rather *what kind* of citizen our educational programs imagine.

I hope that after reading this book you—like me—are left with the sense that schools, beyond teaching children how to read and write, do math problems, and understand science and history, also serve as an inevitable influence on young people's view of the world and, therefore, are a potentially powerful tool that can shape our society for the better.

CHAPTER 1

Changing the Narrative of School

Before becoming a professor of education, I taught 6th, 7th, and 8th grades in the New York City public schools. Like many idealistic new teachers, I entered the profession committed to nothing less than instilling in young people the confidence, knowledge, and skills required to change the world. I wanted my students to treat one another with respect, to challenge injustice when they saw it, and to learn that they were powerful, that they could make a difference, and in the process find deep meaning in their social and professional lives.

Archeem,[1] an African American student in my 7th-grade social studies class, thought otherwise. For my first 6 months in the classroom, Archeem and I were at loggerheads. He was not good at what Denise Pope-Clark calls "doing school."[2] He was a C– student. And I was not yet a skilled teacher. I assumed that by offering Archeem something beyond the superficiality of rote memorization and regurgitation, he would work hard, learn more, and enjoy school. Archeem and many of his classmates, on the other hand, figured that I was a newbie who should be challenged.

THE SCRIPT IN PLACE

My first mistake? I figured that as a teacher, I got to dream up the background material for a script that would then unfold within the humane and educative conditions I had put in motion. New teachers often believe they get to write the script, set the stage, and raise the curtain.

> New teachers often believe they get to write the script, set the stage, and raise the curtain. But students know something that only later becomes evident to the adult in the room: The play has already started.

But students know something that only later becomes evident to the adult in the room: The play has already started. I was entering in Act

III. In Acts I and II, the plot was established, the parts cast, the good guys and bad guys already chosen, the narrative arc long since determined. There were "smart" students and "dumb" ones. There were class clowns and teacher's pets. Kids know how school works long before they enter their first classroom. They see television cartoons about school; they see movies about school; they've heard other children talk about school; they have older siblings who've gone to school. Our culture has already dictated that school entails a timeless, existential battle between the tasks and rules adults impose on the one hand, and students' efforts to preserve their own souls without getting thrown out, on the other hand. They wouldn't describe it that way, but that's the gist of it.

Let me give an example about the difficult-to-break narratives already in place before a teacher even sets foot in the school building. Ask any group of children what happens when a substitute teacher comes to the classroom. What do they say? Mayhem—children move the desks around, change their names, and inform the substitute teacher that their "real" teacher allows them to wander around the room whenever they want and to eat their lunch at 9:15 a.m. In short, they make the life of the substitute a temporary hell. Substitute teachers are clueless and have no idea how to teach, goes the script. Socrates himself could arrive in a 5th-grade classroom for a day. It wouldn't matter. The play is already in motion.

Narratives, however, *can* be rewritten. It takes time, patience, and creativity. Back in my 1st year of teaching, I guessed (having read his school file) that in Archeem's internalized narrative, school was mostly about humiliation. It was the teacher's job to catch him out on not knowing things, and Archeem's job to try to avoid those encounters. I imagined that he recognized the usefulness of acquiring some of the skills and knowledge being taught in school, but that in a larger sense, the connection between what went on in school and his life outside of school was tenuous at best. In those first few months of teaching, neither Archeem nor I knew this yet, but we were both going to find our way outside the dominant narrative of school.

WHAT ARCHEEM TAUGHT ME ABOUT TEACHING

After a week of classes in which we had discussed the civil rights movement, racism, and prejudice in America, all of my students were duly outraged at the injustices perpetrated against Black people throughout history. Students couldn't believe the folly of thinking that someone's intelligence, skills, or rights could be judged by the color of their skin. They sat riveted by excerpts from *Eyes on the Prize* and speeches by Martin Luther King Jr. and Malcolm X. I quickly became aware that although the students were quick to criticize a kind of racism that was already widely reviled in the United States and elsewhere, they failed to carry that critique or moral commitment to any other sphere. I witnessed African American students calling Hispanic students "spic." I saw Archeem and his friend Brian yell "faggot" at a student who didn't share their athletic prowess in dodge ball. When I asked students if they thought people were still prejudged for superficial reasons, they didn't know. I knew something was not working, and I had an idea.

Two weeks earlier, various cities had been observing Gay Pride Week. It was highly controversial, even in New York, and certainly in New York City public schools (this was in the mid-1980s). Despite the explosive nature of the debate, our school principal had agreed to allow an "out" gay teacher to use the second-floor glass display case for posters and newspaper articles about gay pride. But 4 days after the teacher had spent a great deal of his own time on the display, someone or some group of students had smashed in the glass with a chair. The teacher and the principal decided to leave it that way for the time being.

I had a conversation with José, the school janitor. I asked if he would help me by arriving at the beginning of my next social studies class with a ladder and insist that he had to fix a ceiling light which inexplicably would require a power drill and his other noisiest possible tools. He agreed, and as soon as class had started and he began to work, there was no hearing what anyone was saying. I asked students to grab their chairs and to carry them downstairs to the large second-floor hallway where we set up in a circle around the display case with the smashed glass to continue our discussion about racism in America.

I continued to lead the discussion, waiting for what I was not sure would happen. But something happened, and it happened because of Archeem. He had been leaning back in his chair looking characteristically disinterested in the conversation when he suddenly rocked forward and raised his hand. I nodded to Archeem, not sure what would happen next.

"It's like that," Archeem said, pointing to the broken glass. All the students in the circle swung their heads straight to the center of the broken glass.

"Like what?" I asked, hoping I was masking my nervous anticipation of his response.

"Racism is like when you hate someone just because of something about them that you don't even know nothing about."[3] Silence followed. Here was this 13-year-old African American boy somehow, indirectly, standing up for gay people, and perhaps more importantly identifying a contemporary example of prejudice and connecting it to a widely agreed moral standard that called prejudice wrong.

The other students nodded, and a discussion ensued about the connection between different kinds of prejudice. A number of students relied on Archeem's contribution. Latosha started, and I recall her having been on both the giving and receiving end of more than her share of disrespectful taunts:

> "What Archeem said made me realize all the different ways human beings diss each other."
> "Do you think the way southern White people felt about Black people was like how some of us think about gay people?"
> "No, it's not the same—being gay isn't natural."
> "Isn't that what they said about Blacks being free?"
> "No, it's not the same because gay people are disgusting!"
> [laughter].

We hadn't reached a progressive teacher's nirvana by any means, but the conversation had started. For the rest of that week and the next, students researched civil-rights-era documents from the 1950s and 1960s. They read historical opinions about whether Blacks should have the same social and political rights as Whites, and they compared those opinions to contemporary positions (in newspaper articles and legislation) about gay rights. In classes that followed, students continued to refer back to the conversation Archeem had sparked. Two of them wrote a note to the teacher who had created the gay pride display apologizing on behalf of "whomever was too chicken to apologize for themselves."

It became evident to both me and my students that teaching about slavery (racism is bad) or teaching about World War II (Hitler was evil) was too easy. The historical lessons were fine. But the more important message didn't stick: History doesn't stand still, and we can never be complacent about the rights and responsibilities of citizens. If schools are to be instrumental in helping young people engage with the world around them and work to improve it, then the lessons in school have to teach more than a calcified version of past events. Schools need to offer lessons that encourage new interpretations and that lend themselves to contemporary problems. It is relatively common for good teachers to demonstrate to students the potential tyranny of opinion over facts in landmark historical controversies (e.g., the idea that people whose skin is black are not as intelligent or deserving of rights as those whose skin is white). Less clear, however, is whether such lessons give students the skills they need to critically analyze contemporary problems and injustices—the kinds of skills they need in order to be engaged democratic citizens.

> We can never be complacent about the rights and responsibilities of citizens. If schools are to be instrumental in helping young people engage with the world around them and work to improve it, then the lessons in school have to teach more than a calcified version of past events.

Beyond learning history, students need to examine issues that challenge their own assumptions and perspectives. Indeed, that there are not, as of yet, clear "answers" (widespread cultural agreement) on the specific questions makes those issues useful. Back then, having students examine whether gay men should be allowed to serve in the U.S. military, for example, became a more useful issue for discussion and critique than whether African American men should be allowed to serve. The former (at least until this decade) forced difficult analysis and consideration of a variety of viewpoints, while the latter, piggybacking on already-established widespread agreement, failed to do so.

I received two complaints from parents who said they did not want their children discussing gay rights in school. I was willing to weather those complaints, and luckily my principal was similarly undeterred. I had stumbled on one possible, albeit idiosyncratic, way to teach critical thinking. But that was not the only lesson I drew from this experience. From that day on, not exclusively, but regularly, Archeem's attitude toward both school and me changed. There were no miracles, but Archeem seemed to have grown a little bit taller. He began to raise his hand. He participated in discussions. I told other teachers about what Archeem had said and they asked him about it too. When a school assembly included a neighborhood community organizer talking about public housing, Archeem asked me how you get a job like that, working with people in the neighborhood. It seemed in some small way, I no longer fit the role of the teacher trying to catch him not knowing things. As you can tell from my recollections, Archeem became more than a thorn in my novice teacher's side. Together we had changed the narrative.

My experience with Archeem and his classmates taught me something about the complexity of teaching critical thinking when it comes to matters of contemporary concern. But what did this say about the role of schools in democratic societies? What did it say about citizenship?

CHAPTER 2

No Child Left Thinking

Imagine you were visiting a school in a totalitarian nation governed by a single-party dictatorship. Would the educational experiences be markedly different from the ones experienced by children in your local school? That may sound like a facetious question, but I do not intend it that way. It seems plausible that good lessons in multiplication, chemistry, or a foreign language—perhaps with some adjustments for cultural relevance and suitability—would serve equally well in most parts of the world. So if you stepped into a school somewhere on the planet and politely asked to observe some of the lessons, would you be able to tell whether you were visiting a school in a democratic nation or a totalitarian one? Or, conversely, if students from a totalitarian nation were secretly transported to a school in your neighborhood to continue their lessons with new teachers and a new curriculum, would they be able to tell the difference?

The children in your local school would probably learn how to read and write, just like students do in, say, North Korea or China. Students in your local school might learn to add numbers, do fractions, and solve algebraic equations. But that's what students in Uzbekistan learn too. Maybe students in your local school learn not to hit one another, to follow the rules, and not to break any laws. They might sing the national anthem and learn about asteroids and the life cycle of the glowworm. Maybe they even put on plays, learn a musical instrument, and paint pictures. I know of schools in Eritrea and Belarus that do those things too.[1]

My point is that citizens in nondemocratic countries governed by a single-party authoritarian regime, or even a military junta, learn a lot of the same things in school that our children learn. So what goals would be different for schools in a democratic society? For example, do students in democratic countries learn how to participate in public decisionmaking (the kind of participation that is required for democracy to function properly)? Are they taught to see themselves as individual actors who work in concert with others to create a better society? Are they taught the skills they need to think for themselves and to govern collectively?

Most of us would like to believe that they do. While a school in North Korea or China might be teaching students blind allegiance to their nation's leaders and deference to the social and political policies those leaders enact, we would expect that schools in the United States or Canada or Finland would teach students the skills and dispositions needed to evaluate for themselves the benefits and drawbacks of particular policies and government practices. We would not be surprised to learn, for example, that North Korean children are taught to abide by an "official history" handed down by the single-party authoritarian regime. After all, a school curriculum that teaches one unified, unquestioned version of "truth" is one of the hallmarks of totalitarian societies. Democratic citizens, however, should be committed to the principles and values that underlie democracy—such as political participation, free speech, civil liberties, and equal opportunity. Schools might develop these commitments through lessons in the skills of analysis and exploration, free political expression, and independent thought.

TEACHING QUESTIONING—
ESSENTIAL FOR SCHOOLS IN DEMOCRACIES

Much has been written about the purposes of schools in democratic societies, but here is one characteristic that I believe is essential in distinguishing them from their totalitarian counterparts: Schools in democratic societies must teach students how to ask challenging questions—the kinds of questions that are, at times, uncomfortable, the kinds that question tradition. Although most of us would agree that traditions are important, without any questioning there can be no progress. Students need practice in entertaining multiple perspectives and viewpoints on important issues that affect our lives. These issues can sometimes be controversial. But improving society requires embracing that kind of controversy so that citizens can engage in democratic dialogue and work together toward understanding and enacting the most sensible policy decisions possible.

Why would we expect adults, even senators or members of Congress (or Parliament), to be able to intelligently and compassionately discuss different viewpoints in the best interests of their constituents if schoolchildren never or rarely get that opportunity in school? As I discovered through my experience with Archeem and his classmates, students are frequently exposed to historical controversies such as slavery, Nazism, or laws denying voting rights to Blacks or to women—past controversies that are already settled in the minds of all but a small fringe minority of citizens. But those same students are too often shielded from matters that require thoughtful engagement with *today's* competing ideas even though that kind of engagement is exactly what democratic participation requires. Although schools habitually avoid controversial issues, engaging controversial issues may be exactly what is called for. Teaching about injustice might best be achieved through explicit challenges to widespread cultural assumptions rather than through reexamination of historical issues which, by virtue of time, have become unassailable.

We might think this is obvious—that school reformers would do everything possible to ensure that teachers and students have plenty of opportunities to ask these kinds of questions. And our schools often support democratic dispositions in just such ways. But teaching and learning—in both public and independent schools—do not always conform to democratic goals and ideals. Tensions abound, and in recent years some of the very foundations of democratic engagement—such as opportunities for independent thinking and critical analysis—have become less and less common. If being a good democratic citizen requires thinking critically about important social assumptions, then that foundation of citizenship is at odds with recent trends in education policy.

> If being a good democratic citizen requires thinking critically about important social assumptions, then that foundation of citizenship is at odds with recent trends in education policy.

THE ATTACK ON CRITICAL THINKING

The goals of K–12 education have been shifting steadily away from preparing active and engaged public citizens and toward more narrow goals of career preparation and individual economic gain. Pressures from policymakers, business groups, philanthropic foundations, and parents, and a broad cultural shift in educational priorities have resulted in schools being seen primarily as conduits for individual success and, increasingly, lessons aimed at exploring democratic responsibilities have been crowded out. Much of current education reform is limiting the kinds of teaching and learning that can develop the attitudes, skills, knowledge, and habits necessary for a democratic society to flourish.[2]

In many school districts, states, and provinces, ever more narrow curriculum frameworks emphasize preparing students for standardized assessments in math and literacy at the same time that they shortchange the social studies, history, and even basic citizenship education. Moreover, higher-achieving students, generally from wealthier neighborhoods, are receiving a disproportionate share of the kinds of citizenship education that sharpen students' thinking about issues of public debate and concern. This demographic divide—what some scholars have called the "civic opportunity gap"— results in unequal distribution of opportunities to practice democratic engagement.[3]

Curricular approaches that spoon-feed students to succeed on narrow academic tests teach students that broader critical thinking is optional. In other words, the pedagogical challenge I faced with Archeem and his classmates—how to foster thoughtful consideration and analysis of contemporary problems—has all too often been replaced by the single-minded drive to make students better test-takers, rather than better citizens.

The high-stakes testing mandated by No Child Left Behind (NCLB) and Race to the Top (RTTT) legislation has further pushed to the margins educational efforts that challenge students to grapple with tough questions about society and the world. In a study by the Center on Education Policy, 71% of districts reported cutting back on time for other subjects—social studies in particular—to make more space for reading and math instruction.[4] Similarly, research by the Washington-based group Common Core found that two-thirds of public school teachers surveyed report that disciplines such as science, social studies, and art are crowded out of the school day as a direct result of state testing policies.[5] In testimony before the U.S. Senate, historian David McCullough noted that, because of NCLB, "history is being put on the back burner or taken off the stove altogether in many or most schools."[6] An increasing number of students are getting little to no education about how government works, the Constitution, the Bill of Rights, the evolution of social movements, and U.S. and world history. As Peter Campbell, Missouri State Coordinator for FairTest, noted,

The sociopolitical implications of poor black and Hispanic children not learning about the Civil Rights movement, not learning about women's suffrage, not learning about the U.S. Civil War, and not learning about any historical or contemporary instance of civil disobedience is more than just chilling. It smacks of an Orwellian attempt not merely to re-write history, but to get rid of it.[7]

The implications Campbell describes are not limited to poor Black and Hispanic students. Any student being denied knowledge about historical events and social movements misses out on important opportunities to link his or her education to the quintessentially democratic struggles for a better society for all.

I focus on history teaching here, but the trend is not limited to social studies. In many states, virtually every subject area is under scrutiny for any deviation from one single narrative, based on knowable, testable, and purportedly uncontested facts. An English teacher, in a study undertaken by my research team, told us that even novel reading was now prescriptive in her state's rubric: meanings predetermined, vocabulary words preselected, and essay topics predigested. A science teacher put it this way: "The only part of the science curriculum now being critically analyzed is evolution."[8]

As bad as that sounds, omitting lessons that might develop critical thinking skills is still different from forbidding them. But in the book *Pledging Allegiance: The Politics of Patriotism in America's Schools*, I detailed the ways in which schools, districts, states, and even the federal government—in the wake of the 9/11 terrorist attacks—began to implement policies that actually *restrict* critical analysis of historical and contemporary events in the school curriculum.[9] In the worst-case examples, teachers were suspended or fired for teaching lessons on critical analysis of the news or of textbooks, and students were suspended for expressing dissenting opinions on the war in Iraq, organizing "peace clubs," or wearing T-shirts with antiwar quotations. Students and a drama teacher in a Connecticut high school spent months researching, writing, and rehearsing a play they wrote about the Iraq war entitled *Voices in Conflict*. The school administration banned the play on the basis that it was "inappropriate." (In this case, the students went on to perform the play in the spring of 2007 on an off-Broadway stage in New York to impressive critical review.) But efforts to "protect" students from multiple perspectives on historical and contemporary events were not limited to individual cases. State and federal policy followed this trend as well.

In 2003, Tennessee Senator Lamar Alexander introduced his bill, The American History and Civics Education Act, by warning that educators should not expose students to competing ideas in historical texts. Civics, he argued, should be put back in its "rightful place in our schools, so our children can grow up learning what it means to be an American."[10] (For Alexander, what it means to be an American is more *answer* than *question*, it seems.) In April 2008, the Arizona House of Representatives passed SB 1108 specifying that schools whose teachings "denigrate or encourage dissent" from "American values" would lose state funding.[11] More recently, in 2012, the Texas Republican Party platform briefly included language that asserted opposition to "the teaching of critical thinking skills" or lessons that "have the purpose of challenging the student's fixed beliefs."

A more worrisome example, however, comes from Florida. In June 2006, the Florida Education Omnibus Bill included language specifying that "the history of the United States shall be taught as genuine history. . . . American history shall be viewed as factual, not as constructed, shall be viewed as knowable, teachable, and testable."[12] The stated goal of the bill's designers was "to raise historical literacy," with a particular emphasis on the "teaching of facts." For example, the bill requires that only facts be taught when it comes to discussing the "period of discovery" and the early colonies. This led Florida State Representative Shelley Vana, who also served as the West Palm Beach teachers union president, to wonder just "whose facts would they be, Christopher Columbus's or the Indians'?"[13] Florida thus became the first state I know of to ban historical interpretation in public schools, thereby effectively outlawing critical thinking.

Of course, professional historians almost universally regard history as exactly a matter of interpretation; indeed, the competing interpretations are what make history so interesting. Historians and educators alike widely derided the mandated adherence to an official story embodied in the Florida legislation, but the impact of such mandates should not be underestimated. The bill and other similar legislative examples of restricting history lessons to one "true" narrative remain on the books in Florida, Nebraska, Kansas, and other states.

More recently, in the fall of 2014, more than a thousand Jefferson County, Colorado, high school students and hundreds of teachers walked out of classes to protest the school board's efforts to promote "positive" American history and downplay the legacy of civil disobedience and protest. The protests came in the wake of a proposal by the school board to make changes to the Advanced Placement (AP) history curriculum. AP history, the board suggested "should promote citizenship, patriotism, essentials and benefits of the free enterprise system, respect for authority and respect for individual rights. Materials should not encourage or condone civil disorder, social strife or disregard for the law."[14] Responding to the school board's proposal, both teachers and students in Jefferson County boycotted classes, with teachers calling in sick, and students staging a variety of protests outside of schools. One Jefferson County teacher characterized the board's proposal as "an attack on teachers and public education, and a disregard for the needs of our students. . . . It's really, really scary to be a teacher in Jefferson County right now,"[15] while a high school senior, highlighting the irony of students protesting a curriculum that discourages protesting, vowed: "If they don't teach us civil disobedience, we will teach ourselves."[16]

There is a certain irony, evident in the above examples, to the argument that schools in a democratic nation can better prepare students to be democratic citizens by encouraging deference to authority and discouraging lessons about social movements and social change. Reporting on the Colorado protests, *U.S. News and World Report* may have best captured the sentiments of outraged teachers, parents, and students when they wrote that the Jefferson County proposal "isn't about making better citizens. It's about removing the very idea behind good citizenship—the very American premise that we choose our leaders, hold them accountable, demonstrate peacefully to make our views known and to question authority."[17]

> There is a certain irony to the argument that schools in a democratic nation can better prepare students to be democratic citizens by encouraging deference to authority and discouraging lessons about social movements and social change.

At this point, some readers might be thinking that conditions seem restrictive and antidemocratic for students in the public schools, but that, on the whole, many private schools prepare students for a democratic society by offering a broad liberal education that asks students to grapple with difficult and contested policy issues. Evidence indicates otherwise. As the goals for K–12 public education have shifted away from preparing active and engaged public citizens and toward more narrow goals of career preparation and individual economic gain, private schools have, in many ways, led the pack. Pressures from parents, board members, and a broad cultural shift in educational priorities have resulted in schools across the country being seen primarily as conduits for individual success, and lessons aimed at exploring democratic responsibilities have increasingly been crowded out. A steadily growing body of research in the United States now echoes what Tony Hubbard, former director of the United Kingdom's Independent Schools Inspectorate, stated most plainly after reviewing data from an extensive study of British independent schools: Because of the immense pressure to achieve high academic results on exams and elevate schools' prestigious college-entrance rates, independent schools are "overdirected" so that students do not have "sufficient opportunity or incentive to think for themselves." Increasingly following formulas that "spoon-feed" students to succeed on narrow academic tests, independent schools, Hubbard warned, "teach students not to think."[18]

Although the overt examples I've described above that seek to ban critical thinking from classrooms are worrisome, the more insidious developments come from an education-reform movement that makes those efforts unnecessary. So many schools have now become myopically focused on efficiency and accountability that there are simply fewer and fewer opportunities for deeper consideration of important ideas. The relentless focus on testing and "achievement" means that time for in-depth critical analysis of ideas has been diminished. Social studies scholar Stephen Thornton notes that, by critical thinking, school officials too often mean that students should passively absorb as truth the thinking already completed by someone else.[19]

> The hidden curriculum of post-NCLB classrooms became how to please authority and pass the tests, not how to develop convictions and stand up for them.

Current school reform policies and many classroom practices too often reduce teaching and learning to exactly the kind of mindless rule-following that makes students unable to make principled stands that have long been associated with democracy. The hidden curriculum of post-NCLB classrooms became how to please authority and pass the tests, not how to develop convictions and stand up for them. In the next chapter I describe how teachers have become unwilling participants in these efforts.

CHAPTER 3

No Teacher Left Teaching

I began teaching in the New York City Public Schools in 1987 and kept a crude diary of some of my experiences. The entries tend to lean toward tales of Kafkaesque bureaucracy, because taking a detached sociologist's perspective allowed me to laugh rather than lose my mind at some of the obstacles New York City public school teachers face. (To this day, I still advise my teacher education students to keep a simple diary at least during their first few years of teaching.) I wrote about attending required "professional development" sessions in which we were reminded to wear deodorant and not to carry loose change in our pockets because body odor and jangling coins might distract students from their work. I wrote about the time cards in the principal's office that we were supposed to move from the "out" slot to the "in" slot each morning when we arrived and then back to the "out" slot when we left for the day, presumably because teachers couldn't be trusted to call in sick and that if we didn't show up one day, the 35 children in the hallway with no teacher would not be a sufficient indication that something was amiss. I wrote about standing in line at the vice principal's office, waiting to be handed a stack of bus passes for my homeroom students, only to be loudly reprimanded in front of the students for not having filled out the form correctly.

But with all the small indignities I faced as a teacher, for the most part, what I did behind my classroom door was my own business. There was no race to the top. If children were being left behind, legislators had not yet succeeded in directing the daily minutiae of everyday teacher practice. Four years earlier, the *Nation at Risk* report had warned of the "rising tide of mediocrity"[1] and set education reform on the path toward intolerably bland back-to-basics metrics. But schools like mine—an alternative school-within-a-school with a progressive mission—had not yet succumbed to the growing fixation on standardizing classroom practices. It would not be long, however, before standardization rather than teacher professionalization had become the inexorable *cri de guerre* of the reformers.

STANDARDIZATION: A SOLUTION IN SEARCH OF A PROBLEM

Picture the history teacher who draws heavily on his own experience and interests to make past events come alive for his students. Maybe you know him. Students, parents, and colleagues admire him for including in a 20th-century American history course a unit on the role of protest music in the political upheavals of the 1960s. Imagine another teacher whose students study changing immigration policies in urban centers. She uses original documents as fodder for debate. Imagine a math teacher who uses three classes between her units on abstract and linear algebra to have students investigate the biographies of famous mathematicians and postulate how their life's experiences might have influenced their views on mathematics, or another math teacher who leads students in a critical exploration into the origins of algebraic thinking.

These are just four real-life examples of teachers who have now been asked to work closely with their colleagues to "standardize" their curriculum. The problem? Different teachers seem to be assigning different projects, not always covering the same material, and holding students to different expectations with regard to homework, in-class discussions, and choice. The inconsistency, in turn, results not only in variation across what is taught but also in complaints from a handful of parents and students about fairness. The solution? "We would like to develop greater consistency with regard to subject matter and teacher expectations of student work," reads one edict handed down to a group of teachers in one East Coast school. "Please use this development day to establish a common set of standards" begins another from a Midwestern school.

Increasingly, teachers in both public and private schools are being asked to teach the same material in the same way at the same time so that standards and accountability measures can be established. This happens within individual schools everywhere. But the school-by-school standardization efforts are merely local manifestations of a broader top-down bureaucratic obsession with sameness.

Statewide or nationwide dictates about what should be covered in the school curriculum are the primary motivator of homogenization efforts and inevitably have the effect of curbing teachers' abilities to make decisions about what and how they teach. Even global tests such as the Organization for Economic Cooperation and Development's Program for International Student Assessment (PISA) seek, ultimately, to ensure that classroom teaching is the same from one room to another.

> When education reforms turn away from an emphasis on supporting positive conditions of practice and move toward technocratic strategies for "compliance," the profession suffers and so do students.

There is nothing intrinsically wrong with the concept of standards. Most teachers—indeed most professionals in any field—have them. And there is nothing wrong with aiming for some common core of knowledge to be taught in, for example, 9th-grade English. But increasingly, a bottom line for minimum standards and uniformity is being raised to the top of all curricular considerations. As our cultural obsession with standardization and accountability measures is increasingly reflected in our schools, the most common complaint I now hear from both teachers and administrators is the following: *I have been stripped of my professional judgment, creativity, and freedom to make decisions in the best interests of my students.*

When education reforms turn away from an emphasis on supporting positive conditions of practice and move toward technocratic strategies for "compliance," the profession suffers and so do students. Many teachers would echo the sentiments of Gloria, a teacher in a recent study I conducted of the 10th-grade civics curriculum in Ontario. She told us the following:

> In my 22 years of teaching, never have I experienced a climate that has turned all educational problems into problems of measurement until now. Poor citizenship skills? Raise their math and literacy scores. Poor participation? Doesn't matter. Poverty? Inequality? The solution is always always to give the students more tests. These days pedagogically, I feel like I can't breathe.[2]

In classrooms and schools across the country, teachers are under attack, and the public trust that many teachers once enjoyed is threatened

> In classrooms and schools across the country, teachers are under attack, and the public trust that many teachers once enjoyed is threatened by the media, politicians, school boards, and sometimes even by fellow educators.

by the media, politicians, school boards, and sometimes even by fellow educators.

The degree to which "No Child Left Behind" and "Race to the Top" legislation and related reforms have negatively impacted teachers' abilities to act in a professional capacity is only beginning to get the attention it deserves. Finnish educator Pasi Sahlberg calls the kind of school reform that elevates testing and standardization above all other educational considerations GERM (for Global Education Reform Movement). He describes GERM as follows:

> It is like an epidemic that spreads and infects education systems through a virus. It travels with pundits, media and politicians. Education systems borrow policies from others and get infected. As a consequence, schools get ill, teachers don't feel well, and kids learn less.[3]

Not only do kids learn less. What they learn tends to follow prescriptive formulas that match the standardized tests. In the process, more complex and difficult-to-measure learning outcomes get left behind. These include creativity and emotional and social development, but also the kinds of thinking skills associated with robust civic engagement. Teachers' ability to teach critical thinking and students' ability to think and act critically is diminished.

The arguably more well-intentioned but still problematic Common Core State Standards Initiative has further exacerbated the limitations teachers face. Developed in 2009 and 2010 under the auspices of the National Governors Association and the Council of Chief State School Officers, the Common Core State Standards (CCSS) have been adopted by 44 states and the District of Columbia (the widespread participation is due, in part, to the promise of Race to the Top funding for states that adopt the new standards). Although many educators agree that the content of the newer standards has more depth than previous attempts at standardized rubrics, the uniformity they demand inhibits the creativity and flexibility that a truly professional teaching force requires. Moreover, arbitrary requirements based on scant research evidence further call into question the usefulness of attempts to standardize classroom practice by dictating standardized content requirements. For example, CCSS sets specific numerical ratios for the percentage of reading at each grade level that can be fiction or non-fiction (by 12th grade, the goal is 70% nonfiction or "informational"). Pointing out the folly of mobilizing national standards to tell teachers what percentage of their time should be devoted to literature or information, educational historian Diane Ravitch rightly observed that "both can develop the ability to think critically."[4]

Almost every school mission statement these days boasts broad goals related to critical thinking, global citizenship, environmental stewardship, and moral character. Yet beneath the rhetoric, increasingly narrow curriculum goals, accountability measures, and standardized testing have reduced too many classroom lessons to the cold, stark pursuit of information and skills without context and without social meaning—what the late education philosopher Maxine Greene called "mean and repellent facts."[5] It is not that facts are bad or that they should be ignored. But democratic societies require more than citizens who are fact-full. They require citizens who can think and act in ethically thoughtful ways.

If education's democratic goals are to be taken seriously, then we need the kinds of classroom practices that teach students to recognize ambiguity and conflict in "factual" content, to see human conditions and aspirations as complex and contested, and to embrace debate and deliberation as a cornerstone of democratic societies.

DE-PROFESSIONALIZATION AND THE NEW HYPOCRISY

Historically, teaching—especially of the primary years—was a women's profession. That made teachers easy game for paternalistic administrators and board superintendents. Late 19th- and early 20th-century schoolteachers were bound by strict rules governing not only what they taught but also how they taught it, what they should wear, and how they were supposed to conduct themselves outside of the classroom on their own time. Teachers' contracts typically stipulated that (female) teachers were not to keep company with men, get married, travel too far from the school, consume alcohol, or (this is true) spend too much time in ice-cream shops.

Through the latter half of the 20th century, the most egregious examples of teacher infantilization diminished. But the various waves of distrust the public has shown for teachers in the form of "teacher-proof" curriculum continued. The popular Success for All and other scripted instruction programs continue to be implemented in a large number of schools across the country. Scripted instruction programs and dozens of other examples of regimented curricular strategies seek to minimize the risk of bad teaching by standardizing instruction across classrooms.

Sometimes the stripping of professional authority from teachers comes from policies with progressive intentions. Several school districts recently experimented with eliminating penalties for handing in homework late (based on the idea that grades should measure a student's mastery of the material rather than whether they mastered the material at a particular time). Making an end run around teachers' professional judgment, such policies forbid teachers from penalizing students regardless of when they hand in the assignment (which is possibly reasonable in select cases and patently absurd as an applies-to-all directive). An admittedly peculiar example of the trend of de-professionalization, it nonetheless represents accurately the lengths to which many school policies go to restrict teachers' discretion. The more we see such policies enacted, the more far-reaching and troublesome mandated standardized testing becomes, and the less able teachers are to pursue rich educational activities based on individual interests, knowledge, and experience.

Although attempts at de-professionalizing teachers are not new, the newfound hypocrisy is striking. There is a veritable avalanche of calls for "teacher professionalism" in school mission statements, policy documents, and strategic plans, but the professionally respectful rhetoric coexists with newly minted top-down edicts that strip teachers of exactly the curricular and pedagogical decisionmaking authority that allow them to act as professionals. Once teachers might have complained that hard and fast rules dictated from above prevented them from teaching the material that they deem essential or teaching in the way they suspect will be most effective. In a 21st-century twist, it is now the teachers themselves who are often asked to be the architects of their own pedagogical straitjackets. More and more teachers are being asked (and, seeing little choice, are agreeing) to adopt the task of standardizing curriculum or developing accountability strategies that can demonstrate numerical "value-added" comparisons. A growing number of teachers' professional organizations are jumping on board as well.

> In a 21st-century twist, it is now the teachers themselves who are often asked to be the architects of their own pedagogical straitjackets. More and more teachers are being asked to adopt the task of standardizing curriculum

Indeed, attacking teachers' professionalism has become something akin to a national pastime. In the past few years, educators watched in dismay as conservative politicians in Wisconsin, Colorado, New Jersey, and a dozen other states earnestly proclaimed teachers—not hedge-fund managers, subprime mortgage lenders, or bankers—to be the root cause of their respective state's (and the nation's) problems.[6] Teachers, they said, earn too much money, have too much time off, and have too much freedom to teach how they please. They called not only for stripping teachers of their collective bargaining rights, but also for closer monitoring of their work, for merit-based pay schemes, and even for the video surveillance of classrooms and laptops that teachers take home from work. The message behind many of these campaigns is not subtle: Teachers can't be trusted; they need to be monitored and their practices homogenized.

Teaching is not the only service profession under attack. Even doctors are subject to the occasional merit-based pay scheme, asked to compete for their salary based on how many of their patients get better or how many they can treat in an hour. As is the case with teachers, these narrow measures fail to capture the context or the breadth of impact of their professional practice. Unlike doctors, however, who still enjoy relatively high public regard, teachers are the targets of particularly hostile rhetoric and mistrust.

Even in some of the most selective independent schools and the finest public schools that once prided the immense creative and intellectual power of their teaching force, teachers are being asked by administrators to devote their planning efforts to standardizing the curriculum. These are schools where many of the teachers (like the ones I wrote about above) have doctorate degrees or previous careers related to subject areas of special interest that they so freely and passionately incorporated into individualized teaching approaches. These are schools where students used to benefit from the creative and intellectual contributions that highly professional individual teachers made in a myriad of ways. Scarce resources (both time and money) are also squandered on stifling new technology such as curricular mapping software in efforts to further regiment a formerly creative and free-flowing process.

In other words, in the name of standardization and equity (of homework assigned, books read, topics covered, and so on), the teachers are being asked to make themselves interchangeable. As a result, the once passionate, personalized, and professional process of curriculum development and teaching is now characterized by assembly-line malaise in a growing number of schools. And students may lose the opportunity to explore the kind of idiosyncratic topics that demonstrate the richness of inquiry itself and that reflect the kind of diversity of ideas that democratic thinking requires.

CHAPTER 4

How Did This Happen?

There is an old parable about a man searching on his hands and knees under a streetlight. A passerby sees him and asks, "What are you looking for?" Hunched over, eyes not leaving the ground, the man replies, "I've lost my car keys." The kind passerby immediately joins him in his search. After a few minutes searching without success, she asks the man whether he is sure he lost the keys there on the street corner. "No," he replies, pointing down the block, "I lost them over there." Indignant, the woman asks, "Then why are you looking for them here?" The man replies, "Because there's light here."

Behind the onslaught of testing and so-called accountability measures lurks the same perverse logic of the man looking for his keys. We know what matters to most teachers, parents, school administrators, board members, and policymakers. But we are far less sure how to find out whether teachers and schools are successful in teaching what matters. Since we have relatively primitive ways of assessing students' abilities to think, create, question, analyze, form healthy relationships, and work in concert with others to improve their communities and the world, we turn instead to where the light is: standardized measures of students' abilities to decode sentences and solve mathematical problems. In other words, *since we can't measure what we care about, we start to care about what we can measure.*

Of course, I am not being entirely fair. Educational testing enthusiasts do have some ways of measuring, for example, skills related to critical

> Since we can't measure what we care about, we start to care about what we can measure.

thinking. And the reading comprehension tests are evolving to consider not only whether students can understand the words and structure of a particular sentence or paragraph, but also whether they can articulate something about its meaning and implications. But when researchers examine education policies broadly and the classroom practices and habits that follow those policies, it becomes increasingly clear that our educational goals and the methods used to assess educational progress are suffering from an appalling lack of imagination. While lively debate about educational approaches among progressive humanistic educators, critical theorists, poststructuralists, ethical culturalists, and others are widespread, it is interesting to note that educators from all these perspectives are united in their distaste for the mechanistic, technocratic, and dehumanizing teaching and learning that now passes for schooling in many classrooms worldwide.

John Holt may have been the most prescient forecaster of this phenomenon. In his classic 1964 text *How Children Fail*, he wrote that the most significant outcome of the drive for "so-called higher standards in schools is that the children are too busy to think."[1] Teachers have to sacrifice social studies, science, arts, and in-depth analysis of topics in virtually every subject to be able to fit literacy and math drills into the schedule.[2] Along the way, teachers are pushed to the lowest common denominator of content-delivery approaches. Frederick Calder, executive director of the New York State Association of Independent Schools, acknowledged (as I would, too) in a speech to the New York City Guild of Independent Schools, that standardized measures of success have some use for all schools (and notably, independent schools are far less beholden to the demands for standardization than are public schools). But he warned that the kind of standardization (mostly through standardized testing) that "becomes dominant or overarching in a school . . . destroys curricular autonomy, negates the whole point of the Socratic method, and smothers original thought."[3] Calder's concern applies equally, if not more so, to public schools.

WHAT GETS TESTED GETS TAUGHT

There's a saying among teachers: Everybody likes to teach critical thinking, but nobody wants a school full of critical thinkers. Current education reform indicates that policymakers are taking this tongue-in-cheek dictum far too seriously. Although state (and provincial) education rhetoric almost always touts the importance of critical thinking, antibullying and other prosocial behaviors, and democratic engagement, the policies that actually affect classroom teaching tend toward the other direction. Because of a myopic focus on testing in math and literacy, it is becoming more and more difficult to make time for deep consideration of important ideas and controversies.

Students are being asked to learn to read but not to consider what's worth reading. They are being asked to become proficient in adding numbers, but not at thinking about what the answers add up to—how they connect to the society in which they live. In short, students are acquiring bits of knowledge but are not being taught the social, economic, and political relevance of that knowledge.

Since I have conducted a great deal of research in the United States and Canada, I will use those countries as a snapshot of the global standardization trends about which many critics worldwide forewarn. In the United States, entire subject areas—in particular, those that tend to embrace multiple perspectives and complex narratives—have been virtually eliminated from the class schedules of many students to make more room for test preparation in mathematics and literacy. In Canada, a retreat from in-depth problem-based learning; from science, history, and the arts; and even from recess are evident in school boards in almost every province (there are exceptions, such as Prince Edward Island and Manitoba, which have, for the most part, resisted the onslaught of overtesting).

Not only teachers but also school principals are sounding alarms over restrictions on the kind of knowledge that is being taught to children. The Canadian Principals Association went to the unusual step of issuing a "statement of concern" regarding student testing and its impact on thinking and learning. School-based administrators throughout Canada, they wrote, "are increasingly concerned that current policies and practices on student testing are leading to . . . a secretive or unintended shift of priorities to focus on a narrow range of student knowledge and literacy/numeracy skills."[4]

Have education policies, boards, or individual schools forbidden teachers to teach other subject areas or to encourage students to critically examine ideas in deep and meaningful ways? Have they forbidden students to recognize the importance of their education in the context of the common good and their relationships to other human beings? No. (Well, at least not in most places—there was that frightening example from Florida that I described earlier.) But a plain fact that every teacher, student, and school principal knows seems to elude most proponents of a test-based curriculum. As Jack Jennings, CEO of the Washington, DC–based Center on Education Policy, notes:

> What gets tested gets taught. Under No Child Left Behind [and he could be talking about standardized testing and accountability measures in any

country or locality], there is reading and math and then there is everything else. And because there is so much riding on the reading and math
included on state tests, many schools have cut back time on other important subject areas, which means that some students are not receiving
a broad curriculum.[5]

To the extent that a broad curriculum continues to be taught, in-
depth thinking about the curriculum as it relates to democratic concerns has been greatly circumscribed. In many ways, big and small,
school practices are in danger of becoming irrelevant to anything but
the narrowest of educational goals. Engaging students in thinking
about the world beyond the bubble-form answer sheet and their role
in shaping the future of that world, is, in too many schools, an extra-
curricular activity.

THE TEST SCORES THAT ATE HUMANITY

The cultural shifts that have led to overemphasizing standards and accountability measures in a narrow range of skills (basic numeracy and
literacy) result in an intellectually emaciated curriculum and reduced
professional autonomy for teachers. But the most disturbing loss concerns the diminished value attributed to any educational activity that
standardized tests do not measure—in other words, the educational
goals that aren't under the streetlight. When activities that are important for the development of well-educated citizens other than mathematics and literacy instruction remain part of the school experience,
they now are often justified by being linked to better standardized test
scores. Arts? Maybe, if there's time and money left after test prep or if
it can be demonstrated that participating in the arts raises mathematical literacy or literary prowess. Recess? Just enough so children can
concentrate better on mathematics and reading instruction (sometimes recess is cut altogether—in particular for those students who are
not performing well on the tests). Most educators will be able to name
five or six activities that have been either curtailed or refashioned so
that their existence can be justified by citing evidence that engaging
in these activities leads to better test scores or academic performance.
One example stands out beyond what might have been imagin-
able a decade ago. The federally funded School Breakfast Program
enables individual states to provide free breakfast for more than 7

million schoolchildren who would otherwise go hungry. Deeply committed volunteers and employees work in thousands of such programs nationwide. But a quick round-up of the websites that describe the various programs reveals a troubling development. Nearly all of these programs feel the need to justify feeding hungry children by citing research that demonstrates a link between hunger and low test scores. The Baltimore program proudly cites research that proclaims, "Students who increased their breakfast participation showed significantly improved math grades." Maryland's Meals for Achievement program observes that "classroom breakfast has a positive impact on Maryland School Performance and Assessment Program (MSPAP) scores and grades." The Massachusetts program assures the public that "participation in the School Breakfast Program is associated with significant improvements in academic functioning among low-income elementary school children." This trend is not limited to the United States. In Ottawa, Canada, the Q & A section of the Ottawa School Breakfast Program website lists as their number one question, "Why is the school breakfast program important?" The answer takes away any doubt about the need for educational programs to mold themselves in the image of math and reading score improvement vehicles:

> Children who arrive at school hungry do not perform well in the classroom. Numerous studies have shown that students who are fed are more alert, develop greater self-esteem, have better attendance, and fewer discipline problems. Children who receive a healthy, nutritious head start to the day show a marked improvement in academic achievement.[6]

I should not need to point out that feeding hungry children because they don't have enough food to eat and are hungry should be all the justification any of these programs need. But gaining public and governmental support for such a program requires evidence that it will help children pass the test. (By the way, if you are a social scientist, you may wonder about the researchers who are apparently *studying* children to find out whether alertness and food deprivation are inversely related. Who comprises the control groups in these studies? Are they starving some kids and then finding out that they don't do so well on tests?)

My intention is not to disparage these programs and the wonderful work they do. Program staff are trying to attract funding in a way that speaks to funders and the general public. But if educators cannot even provide food to children who are hungry without linking such actions to increased standardized test scores, then the battle for the hearts and minds of the public when it comes to educational goals such as critical thinking, creativity, and civic engagement is enormous.

But it is not impossible. Teaching what we care about and drawing on our passions and creative ambitions should not be the exception in our schools.

RECLAIMING THE PROFESSION:
TEACHER PROFESSIONALISM AND DEMOCRATIC THINKING

The U.S. Department of Education continues to list teacher shortages in almost every state. It turns out that 50% of teachers leave the profession within their first 5 years, amounting to 1,000 teachers leaving teaching for greener pastures *every day*. Contrast that with Finland (which, as Pasi Sahlberg notes, has, for the most part, resisted the "GERM" he wrote about). "We give our teachers a lot of freedom in their work," said Henna Virkkunen, Finland's Minister of Education. "This autonomy contributes to the popularity of the profession. . . . After that, it's easy for us when we have the right people." Indeed, in 2010, Finland had over 6,600 applicants for 660 primary school teacher education slots.[7] Getting and keeping the right people in the teaching profession will require a kind of public respect for teachers that is now sorely lacking in North America.

Yet conveying the importance of a rich educational experience beyond test scores to students, parents, policymakers, and the public should not be an insurmountable task, despite the recent attacks on the profession. While it is true that a significant portion of the U.S. public harbors mistrust and sometimes disdain for the profession of teaching (fueled by anti-teacher animus from media commentators such as those on Fox News), it is also true that a majority of us have had teachers who made an enormous positive impact on our lives, and most parents believe that teaching is about more than narrow tests of performance on myopic measures of school success. Increasing numbers of teachers, administrators, and a large number of university professors recognize the need to push back against the narrowing of the school curriculum to only those subjects that are under the streetlight.

In fact, education goals—particularly in democratic societies—have always been about more than narrow measures of success, and teachers have often been called upon and appreciated for instilling in their students a sense of purpose, meaning, community, compassion, integrity,

> *Of course* children need to learn to read and to write and to add numbers. But they also need to know how to connect that knowledge to matters of social concern—that is, to their roles as democratic citizens.

imagination, and commitment. Every teacher accomplishes these more artful and ambiguous tasks in different ways. Teaching for democratic thinking requires the pursuit of these multiple perspectives and approaches.

Much as Darwin's theory of natural selection depends on genetic variation, any theory of democracy depends on a multiplicity of ideas. If things are going to improve, parents, administrators, and politicians alike will have to acknowledge that educators in a democratic society have a responsibility to create learning environments that teach students how to think, how to critically analyze multiple perspectives, and how to develop the passion for participation in the kind of dialogue on which a healthy democracy relies. But only those teachers who are free to work as professionals, exploiting their own interests and passions, have any chance of achieving these goals.

The first step is to convince both educators and the broader public that, although teaching the basics is important, it is *not* enough. *Of course* children need to learn to read and to write and to add numbers. But they also need to know how to connect that knowledge to matters of social concern—that is, to their roles as democratic citizens. And to enable children to achieve this goal, talented teachers need the freedom and professional autonomy to work the magic of their art in a myriad of different ways that defy standardization and regimentation of practice. Education philosopher John Dewey beautifully articulated this point more than a century ago:

> The school is an institution in which the child is, for the time, to live—to be a member of a community life in which he feels that he participates, and to which he contributes. This fact requires such modification of existing methods as will insure that the school hours are regarded as much a part of the day's life as anything else, not something set apart; and the school house, as for the time being, a home, not simply a place to go in order to learn certain things.[8]

For Dewey, the school was to serve as a place where children implicitly learn the connections between the knowledge and skills they are gaining in the classroom and the contributions they could make with that knowledge and those skills to the social and civic life of the community. The goal of schooling, he wrote, "must be such as to enable the child to translate his powers over into terms of their social equivalencies; to see what they mean in terms of what they are accomplishing in social life.[9] There are already a growing number of teachers, policymakers, researchers, parents, and students who recognize that largely unfulfilled promise of a kind of schooling that embraces a democratic way of life as one of its core principles.

I have one final comment about the parable of the streetlight. Although, of course, shining a spotlight in an area where one did not lose one's keys will not uncover the missing keys, the effects are actually worse than not finding what one is looking for. When one area is illuminated, anything outside the circle of light is simultaneously darkened. If you have ever walked in the woods at night with a flashlight, you will remember your blindness to anything beyond the light. If the man and woman in the story shifted their gaze from beneath the streetlight to where the keys actually lay, they would likely be blinded (at first) in the newfound darkness; it would seem darker than if they had not been staring in the light for so long. It is the same with our spotlight on mathematics and literacy testing, on standardization of the curriculum and of teachers' practices. The first step to drawing attention to what could be discovered with a broader walk in the woods might be to dim the light that now shines so relentlessly bright.

What would it take for schools to prepare students for democratic citizenship? What vision of "good" citizenship can students pursue? In the following chapter, I explore school-based efforts that go beyond test preparation and standardized teaching in math and literacy to seek answers to these questions. The activities and programs I describe endeavor to tie the school curriculum to community goals in order to nurture citizenship skills and habits. As you will see, however, research that investigates these programs' accomplishments and shortcomings yields surprising results.

CHAPTER 5

What Kind of Citizen?

Let no one attempt with small gifts of charity to exempt themselves from the great duties imposed by justice.

—Pope Pius XI, *Divini Redemptoris*

Ask people of any nation if they think children should learn how to be good citizens and most will say, "Of course!" Ask them if teaching children to get involved in their community is a good idea, and, again, most will assure you that it is. But when the questions go deeper, the easy consensus starts to fray. Beyond the clichés, when educators wrestle with the details of what will actually be taught about civic values, civic participation, peace and war, nationhood and citizenship, global communities and global economies, polite conversation gives way to heated exchanges.

Even amidst our current educational preoccupation with the narrow curriculum goals that I described in the preceding chapters, many teachers, principals, parents, academics, and policymakers continue to champion school activities and programs that go beyond the three R's because they believe that teaching children good citizenship skills is important. Beyond classes in civics and government, you may recognize character education programs like 8 Keys of Excellence, Character Counts!, or Character First! (I don't know why so many character education program names end in an exclamation point!). Or you may know of service-learning programs that seek to connect academic work to community-based experiences. All of these are instances of educators caring about more than just test scores in reading and math.

On the one hand, I find it heartening that people are still talking about the importance of citizenship, particularly the values associated with community and participation. On the other hand, just because lots of people are talking about good citizenship doesn't mean they're on the same page about what, exactly, schools should do. I've attended meetings—some with education scholars, others with school practitioners, and others with parents—where the head-nodding agreement on the importance of teaching good citizenship makes it seem like this is so clearly a universal goal that it barely needs to be discussed at all.

But when the discussions get more detailed—what should we actually do to teach good citizenship?—people's innermost values and beliefs about children and the future of society are brought to the surface. Teachers, administrators, parents, and policymakers hold an assortment of different and sometimes contradictory beliefs. It should not be surprising, then, that school programs that seek to teach good citizenship represent a similarly broad variety of goals and practices. Some programs are based on the belief that good citizens show up to work on time, follow the rules, and pay taxes. Others hope to teach students to be nice to their neighbors and to act decently to the people around them. A few programs seek to teach students to help shape social policy on behalf of those in need. Proponents of these programs want students to become aware of the difficulties involved in changing the circumstances that lead to rivers or parks being dirty or to individuals and families being hungry. When educators, policymakers, politicians, and community activists pursue democratic citizenship, they do so in many different ways and toward many different ends.

Students are no more in agreement on what good citizenship means than are adults. During focus-group interviews with students about what it means to be a good citizen, one offered, "Someone who's active and stands up for what they believe in. If they know that something's going on that is wrong, they go out and change it." But another student from a different school expressed the view that to be a good citizen, you need to "follow the rules, I guess . . . even though you want to break them sometimes," adding, after a small pause, ". . . like cattle."[1]

Rather than supporting the idea that schools should teach one kind of citizenship over another, you may believe that schools shouldn't be in the business of shaping beliefs and behaviors at all—that maybe the development of civil behavior or habits of civic participation should be left to parents, churches, or youth groups, and that teachers should stick to "the basics." But even if students studied only math and literacy all day long, citizenship lessons

> When educators, policymakers, politicians, and community activists pursue democratic citizenship, they do so in many different ways and toward many different ends.

would still be present. Students generally spend more hours in the company of teachers than parents, and schools are brimming with a "hidden curriculum" of behavior and norms of engagement.

We all were taught various lessons about citizenship in school, such as how to get along with others, how to fulfill our responsibilities in the classroom and the broader community, and how to avoid the kinds of nefarious activities that result in an unpleasant encounter with the school principal or vice principal. Schools are chock full of these kinds of *implicit* lessons about being a good citizen. Even without specific classes in citizenship, government, character, or life skills, how the classroom is organized, the architecture of the school, the daily schedule, as well as the procedures and rules all have embedded lessons about how one should best behave in order to be a good community member, classmate, student, and so on.

Although these implicit lessons in citizenship are important, I want to discuss some research on school programs that make *explicit* claims about teaching students how to be good citizens in democratic societies.

THREE KINDS OF CITIZENS

My longtime colleague Joe Kahne and I spent the better part of a decade studying a broad variety of programs that aimed to develop good citizenship skills among youth and young adults. Many of these programs were very explicit about the specific needs of citizens in democratic societies, and so we began to talk openly about the needs of *democratic* citizens. Over the years, we've written a number of articles about those studies, and parts of this chapter and the two following chapters are adapted from work we co-authored. Many of these articles are available online if you're interested in the detailed (and sometimes technical) research.[2] In study after study, we came to similar conclusions: The kinds of goals and practices commonly represented in school programs that hope to foster good democratic citizenship usually have more to do with voluntarism, charity, and obedience than with democracy. In other words, "good citizenship" to many educators means listening to authority figures, dressing neatly, being nice to neighbors, and helping out at a soup kitchen—not grappling with the kinds of social policy decisions that every citizen in a democratic society needs to learn how to do.

From our studies and with the help of teachers and program leaders, we identified three visions of "good" citizens that help capture the lay of the land when it comes to citizenship education: the Personally Responsible Citizen; the Participatory Citizen; and the Social-Justice Oriented Citizen.[3] These ideas about good citizenship are like three different answers to this question: *What kind of citizen do we need to support an effective democratic society?* In mapping the terrain that surrounds answers to this question, we found that these visions of citizenship were particularly helpful in making sense of the different programs we studied. As Table 5.1 illustrates, they can serve as a helpful guide to uncovering the variety of assumptions that fall under the idea of citizenship education.

Each vision of citizenship reflects a distinct set of goals. They are not cumulative. Programs that promote social justice–oriented citizens do not necessarily promote personal responsibility and participatory citizenship, although a given program might simultaneously further more than one of these sets of priorities. For instance, while a curriculum designed principally to promote personally responsible citizens will generally look quite different than one that focuses primarily on developing capacities and commitments for participatory citizenship, it is possible for a given curriculum to further both goals. Although such overlap may occur, drawing attention to the distinctions between these visions of citizenship is important. It highlights the value of examining the underlying goals and assumptions that drive different educational programs and that, ultimately, represent different visions of the "good" citizen.

The Personally Responsible Citizen

The personally responsible citizen acts responsibly in his or her community by picking up litter, giving blood, recycling, and staying out of debt. Personally responsible citizens pay taxes, obey laws, and help those in need during crises such as snowstorms or floods. They might contribute to charitable causes such as a food or clothing drive and volunteer to help those less fortunate, whether in a soup kitchen or a senior center. Both those in the character education movement and many of those who advocate community service would emphasize this vision of good citizenship. Programs that seek to develop personally responsible citizens hope to build character and personal responsibility by emphasizing honesty, integrity, self-discipline, and hard work.[4] The Character Counts! Coalition, for example, advocates teaching

Table 5.1. Kinds of Citizens

	Personally Responsible Citizen	Participatory Citizen	Social Justice–Oriented Citizen
Description	Acts responsibly in the community	Active member of community organizations and/or improvement efforts	Critically assesses social, political, and economic structures
	Works and pays taxes Picks up litter, recycles, and gives blood	Organizes community efforts to care for those in need, promote economic development, or clean up environment	Explores strategies for change that address root causes of problems
	Helps those in need, lends a hand during times of crisis	Knows how government agencies work	Knows about social movements and how to effect systemic change
	Obeys laws	Knows strategies for accomplishing collective tasks	Seeks out and addresses areas of injustice
Sample action	Contributes food to a food drive	Helps to organize a food drive	Explores why people are hungry and acts to solve root causes
Core assumptions	To solve social problems and improve society, citizens must have good character; they must be honest, responsible, and law-abiding members of the community	To solve social problems and improve society, citizens must actively participate and take leadership positions within established systems and community structures	To solve social problems and improve society, citizens must question and change established systems and structures when they reproduce patterns of injustice over time

Source: Westheimer, J., & Kahne, J. (2004). What kind of citizen? The politics of educating for democracy. *American Educational Research Journal, 41*(2), 237–269.

students to "treat others with respect . . . deal peacefully with anger . . . be considerate of the feelings of others . . . follow the Golden Rule . . . use good manners" and so on. They want students not to "threaten, hit, or hurt anyone [or use] bad language."[5] Other programs that seek to develop personally responsible citizens hope to nurture compassion by engaging students in volunteer activities. As illustrated in the mission of the Points of Light Foundation, these programs hope to "help solve serious social problems" by "engag[ing] more people more effectively in volunteer service."[6]

The Participatory Citizen

Participatory citizens actively participate in the civic affairs and the social life of the community at local, state, and national levels. Advocates of this vision emphasize preparing students to engage in collective, community-based efforts. Educational programs designed to support the development of participatory citizens focus on teaching students about how government and other institutions (such as community-based organizations and churches) work and about the importance of planning and participating in organized efforts to care for those in need, for example, or in efforts to guide school policies. Skills associated with these collective endeavors–such as how to run a meeting–are also seen as important since collective community work helps to build relationships, common understandings, and trust.[7] While the personally responsible citizen would contribute cans of food for the poor, the participatory citizen might organize the food drive.

The Social Justice–Oriented Citizen

A third image of a good citizen, and perhaps the perspective that is least commonly pursued, is of individuals who know how to critically assess multiple perspectives. They are able to examine social, political, and economic structures and explore strategies for change that address root causes of problems. We called this kind of citizen the Social Justice–Oriented Citizen because the programs fostering such citizenship emphasize the need for citizens to be able to think about issues of fairness, equality of opportunity, and democratic engagement. The justice-oriented citizen shares with the participatory citizen an emphasis on collective work related to the life and issues of the community. But justice-oriented programs give priority to enabling students to be thoughtfully informed about a variety of complex social issues, think independently, and look for ways to improve society. These programs are less likely to emphasize the need for charity and volunteerism as ends in themselves, and more likely to teach about ways to effect systemic change. If *Participatory Citizens* organize the food drive and *Personally Responsible Citizens* donate food, the *Social Justice–Oriented Citizens*—some might also call them critical thinkers—ask why people are hungry, then act on what they discover.

If *Participatory Citizens* organize the food drive and *Personally Responsible Citizens* donate food, the *Social Justice–Oriented Citizens*—some might also call them critical thinkers—ask why people are hungry, then act on what they discover.

AN INTERLUDE FOR REFLECTION

I hope at this point in the book the description of the three kinds of citizens offers a way to look at programs with which you might be familiar. Consider these activities:

- If you work in a service-learning program or a character-education program, teach a civics class, or facilitate community-service activities, try discussing the kinds of goals represented by the three visions of the "good" citizen" with your colleagues. Do you or your colleagues emphasize one or more of these kinds of goals?
- If you are a school administrator or a policymaker, think about whether school or districtwide policies enable or constrain particular visions of citizenship or favor some goals over others.
- If you are a prospective teacher or a student, reflect on some of your own educational experiences. Were you or are you being taught to be the kind of citizen that is personally responsible, participates, and/or thinks critically about root causes of problems and their solutions?
- If you are a parent or an interested community member and you imagine your ideal society, what kinds of citizens would populate its towns and cities?

THE MANY FACES OF "GOOD" CITIZENSHIP

Philosophers, historians, and political scientists have long debated which conceptions of citizenship would best advance democracy.[8] In large part, this diversity of perspectives occurs because the stakes are so high. Having an opinion on what makes a "good citizen" is really another way of conveying one's idea about what makes a good society. If we gathered 10 people right now and sat down over dinner to discuss what schools should teach about being a good citizen, we would find points of agreement, certainly, but also many points of contention.

> Having an opinion on what makes a "good citizen" is really another way of conveying one's idea about what makes a good society.

Even if we confined our conversation to ideas about good *democratic* citizens, we would have quite a lot of variation. For some of our imaginary guests at our imaginary party, a commitment to democracy might be synonymous with a promise to protect freedoms, while for others democracy might be primarily about equality or equality of opportunity. To some, civil society is the key, while to others, free markets are the great hope for a democratic society. To some, good citizens in a democracy volunteer, while to others they take active parts in political processes by voting, protesting, and working on political campaigns.

These disputes are not new. In the 1920s and 1930s, ideas about democratic education rooted in commitments to improving society through collective action achieved a wide hearing among educators. Known as "social reconstructionists," these reformers emphasized teaching students to be active participants in a democratic civic community, able to envision, articulate, and act on conceptions of a better world.

Harold Rugg, for example, focused on critical analysis of major social issues and institutions. He wanted students to examine "Problems of the 'market' and its historical development," "How the press developed its influence at various times in our growth," and "The history of labor problems; movements for the increase of cooperation between capital and labor; problems of wages, hours, living conditions."[9] Rugg developed a series of textbooks and learning materials that sold more than 1 million copies during the 1930s. The goal of this series, and of the social reconstructionists more generally, was to engage students in the analysis of major institutions and social issues so that social problems, causes, and ways to respond could be identified. The Rugg series of textbooks sold well until the start of World War II when nationalist sentiments made critiques of American society unpopular. Rugg's texts became a lightning rod for the rising anticommunist power in politics.[10] Some of today's programs that embrace the kind of social-justice vision of citizenship I described above would have likely been welcomed by Rugg and his colleagues.[11]

Other progressive-era curriculum theorists and educational reformers were attracted to experience-based approaches that emphasized projects tied to social needs. Like Rugg and his colleagues, they wanted schools to teach a kind of social justice–oriented citizenship that included critical analysis. But they emphasized the role of participation in actual experiences. "As the purposeful act is thus the typical unit of the worthy life in a democratic society," wrote William Kilpatrick in 1918, "so also should it be made the typical unit of school procedure."[12] These educators believed that experiential activities could awaken students' political and social conscience. They wanted to create "miniature communities" through which students learned the value of working together in order to identify and respond to problems that they confronted.[13] They believed in a blend of both participatory and social justice–oriented citizenship.

This focus on communal undertakings tied to social needs led many progressive-era educators to promote what they called the "core curriculum."[14] The "core" was designed to place multidisciplinary analysis and action regarding social problems and themes from social life at the heart of students' school experience. Students in some schools that adopted the core curriculum spent between 2 and 3 hours a day in core classes initiating projects where they examined and responded to major issues facing both individuals and their community. For instance, they studied and initiated programs of environmental improvement; did work with the elderly, orphans, and infants; and examined safety issues in the home and community.[15]

Of course, personally responsible citizenship is not a new idea either. Bill Bennett, former secretary of education under Ronald Reagan, once wrote that "a democracy depends on schools that help to foster a kind of character which respects the law and . . . respects the value of the individual."[16] History is also full of examples of school programs that sought to teach children individual reliance, character, and respect for the law. These programs tend to be more interested in preserving social traditions than in changing them. In the next chapter I will examine personally responsible citizenship programs more closely.

CHAPTER 6

Personally Responsible Citizens

There is a parable about a small village by a river. One day the villagers were working in fields by the river when a woman notices a baby floating downstream. She yells out and someone runs into the river and rescues the baby. One neighbor provides clothes, another food, and so on. The next day, the same villagers are working by the river. They see two babies floating downstream and rescue them. The following day it's four babies and after that eight. Within a short time, practically the entire village is wading into the water, rescuing babies, clothing them, feeding them, trying to find others who will house them, and then returning to rescue more. After a week of rescuing hundreds of babies, one villager yells out, "Hey! Why don't we go upstream and find out how all these babies are falling into the river?" The others quickly reject the suggestion, saying that there are too many babies in the river, and everyone should continue rescuing them lest they drown.

The moral of the story? Volunteering and providing services for those in need is important. But providing those services without also looking at the root causes of the problem—looking upstream—makes little sense. Personal responsibility and even participating with others to organize a response to a social problem is admirable but inadequate if we don't also look at the structural causes that are creating the need for direct service in the first place.

WHY PERSONAL RESPONSIBILITY IS NOT ENOUGH

Currently, the vast majority of school programs that take the time to teach citizenship are the kind that emphasize either good character—including the importance of volunteering and helping those in need—or technical knowledge of legislatures and how government works. Far less common are school programs that teach students

to think about root causes of problems or challenge existing social,
economic, and political norms as
a way to strengthen democracy.
When we deny students the opportunity to consider paths for change
that involve a critical examination
of collective social policy questions
(and not just individual character),

> When we deny students the
> opportunity to consider paths
> for change, we also betray an
> important principle of demo-
> cratic governance: the need for
> citizens to be able to engage
> in informed critique and make
> collective choices.

we also betray an important principle of democratic governance: the
need for citizens to be able to engage in informed critique and make
collective choices.

Remember my question at the beginning of Chapter 2? How
would you know the difference between educational experiences in
two schools—one in a totalitarian nation and one in a democratic one?
Both the totalitarian nation and the democratic one might engage students in volunteer activities in the community—perhaps by picking
up litter from a nearby park or helping out at a busy intersection near
a school or a senior-citizen center. Government leaders in a totalitarian regime would be as delighted as those in a democracy if their
young citizens learned the lessons put forward by many of the proponents of personally responsible citizenship—don't do drugs, show up
to work on time, give blood, help others during a flood, recycle. These
are all desirable traits for people living in a community. But they are
not about democratic citizenship. In fact, voluntarism and kindness
can be used to avoid thinking about politics and policy altogether.

Some conceptions of personal responsibility—for example, obedience and loyalty—may even work against the kind of independent
thinking that effective democracy requires. There is nothing inherent-
ly *democratic* about the traits of a personally responsible citizen, and
there are practices at times specifically *undemocratic* that are associated
with programs that rely exclusively on notions of personal responsibility. When we fail to consider personal responsibility within a broader social context, we risk advancing mere civility or docility rather
than democracy.

It is not at all clear that character education, as it is most often
implemented in schools, will solve
deep-seated social problems unless
accompanied by important lessons in

> When we fail to consider
> personal responsibility within a
> broader social context, we risk
> advancing mere civility or docility
> rather than democracy.

critical analysis and reasoning. As John Holt observes in *How Children Fail*, "Schools tend to mistake good behavior for good character."[1] When we consider the implications for democracy, the consequences become even more stark. Character traits such as honesty, integrity, and responsibility for one's actions are certainly valuable for becoming good neighbors. But, on their own, they are not about democracy. This fact should raise concern when politicians promote voluntarism and charity as an alternative to social policy and organized government action. The phrase "a thousand points of light," for example, asks us to imagine people everywhere engaged in charitable efforts to respond to those in need. There's nothing wrong with that, of course. But if young people understand these actions as a kind of noblesse oblige—a private act of kindness performed by the privileged—and fail to examine the deeper structural causes of social ills, then the thousand points of light risk becoming a thousand points of the status quo. Citizenship in a democratic society requires more than kindness and decency. Unfortunately, the hidden curriculum of too many character education programs is how to be nice and please authority, not how to develop convictions and stand up for them.

Focusing only on direct service and charity while ignoring systemic problems does little to stem the flow of babies in the river. These are easy lessons to miss. A few years ago, I attended the anniversary of a homeless shelter and soup kitchen in lower Manhattan. This was a well-established center that had strong historic roots in the community and, accordingly, there were television and newspaper reporters present as well as a large number of community activists, volunteers, and donors. The executive director stood to welcome everyone and, beaming, told the crowd that the shelter was now serving three times as many people as it had the previous year. He meant well, of course, and the work of his staff and the center deserves recognition. But I was still left wondering whether this was good news or bad news.

School programs that focus exclusively on personal responsibility fail to give students the opportunity to consider broader-scale, social-policy solutions. Programs that privilege individual acts of compassion and kindness often neglect the importance of social action, political engagement, and the pursuit of just and equitable policies. *The vision promoted by many of these school initiatives is one of citizenship without politics or collective action—a commitment to individual service, but not to democracy.*

Perhaps, though, an emphasis on character or voluntary service will draw students into civic participation and make them more likely to participate politically, in democratic ways. Is that what happens? Studies of various forms of civic and political engagement among young people indicate that it may not be. For example, while voter participation and other forms of political engagement among youth and young adults have fallen sharply in the last few decades, a study commissioned by the National Association of Secretaries of State found that 94% of those aged 15–24 believed that "the most important thing I can do as a citizen is to help others."[2] In a very real sense, youth seem to be learning that citizenship does not require government, politics, or even collective endeavors. We're teaching students to rescue, clothe, and feed the babies, but not to seek ways to prevent them from ending up in the river in the first place.

> Youth seem to be learning that citizenship does not require government, politics, or even collective endeavors. We're teaching students to clothe and feed the babies, but not to seek ways to prevent them from ending up in the river in the first place.

ARE EVALUATIONS ASKING THE WRONG QUESTIONS?

If you are a researcher or a policymaker or if you make funding decisions based on program evaluations, you might also find the following worrisome: Evaluations of school-based citizenship education are biased toward individual-character-based ideas of personally responsible citizenship. They showcase the same penchant for individualistic rather than collective solutions to social problems. Program-evaluation research overwhelmingly steers clear from investigating students' understandings of organized movements, both historical and contemporary, and the ways in which government and corporate sectors constrain and enable solutions to social problems.

Common survey questions administered to students before and after they participate in various programs use what is a called a five-point Likert scale (ranging from strongly disagree to strongly agree) to ask students whether they feel it is *their* responsibility to take care of people in need, help others without being paid, recycle cans and bottles, and so on. These questions (and many more like them) emphasize individual actions or a vague sense of individual participation and charitable acts. They ignore other possible levers for change in a democracy, such as working to shape government policy on behalf of those in need.[3]

These same surveys do not ask students questions that address issues such as whether there are enough jobs that pay decent wages for anyone who wants to work or how society should respond if there are not. They ignore the fact that government policy, corporate behavior, and systemic structural challenges represent important concerns for citizens who hope to improve society.

Another question frequently posed to students further illustrates this point. This question, posed on large-scale surveys of service-learning programs asks students whether problems of pollution and toxic waste are "everyone's responsibility including mine" or "not my responsibility." Do you see anything wrong with this question? Toxic waste is rarely the responsibility of individuals but rather the result of industrial pollution. I doubt that whole cities of individuals are running down to the local river, cutting open their flashlight batteries and dumping in the toxic contents. It doesn't matter whether you believe that a reduction in toxic waste can best be achieved through government regulation or voluntary corporate codes of practice. You will probably agree that a focus on individual responsibility misses the point. Social action, corporate responsibility, or government action are all reasonable levers for substantive change, but each is obscured by a narrow focus on the individual.

Evaluations rarely measure other aspects of citizenship, such as a group's ability to accomplish a task or an individual's capacity to organize a group. The result is that programs that might be successful in teaching students how to analyze root causes of problems or organize others to change an unjust law may be deemed failures if they did not also focus on ensuring that students want to volunteer in a soup kitchen or pick up litter. Program evaluations and other forms of research that measure only a narrow range of possible civic outcomes (e.g., personal responsibility) are incomplete at best and destructive at worst. These kinds of evaluations often dictate which programs get funding and which do not, creating a funding-driven, evidence-based feedback cycle in which programs that focus on individual behavior (personally responsible citizenship) gain support at the expense of those that teach students critical analysis and encourage deeper understandings of social policy and reform.

*   *   *

In Chapter 5, I described the three kinds of citizens often envisioned by school-based practices and programs, and in this chapter, I outlined what I see as the shortcomings of programs with an exclusive focus on individual character or personal responsibility. We would all like to live among people who are kind and considerate, generous and honest, and I'm all for schools doing their part to encourage those character traits among young people. But democratic citizenship requires more. That's where the other two visions of the "good" citizen come in to play.

> We would all like to live among people who are kind and considerate, generous and honest. But democratic citizenship requires more.

People who write about citizenship and democracy, and educators who develop citizenship education programs often conflate these two visions of citizenship. If we get kids to actively participate in the community, the thinking goes, then they will gain an understanding of some of the structural or root causes of problems that need attention. Conversely, if students are taught about social injustices, social movements, protest, and change, they will want to get involved in order to improve society. If you want to read about research that calls these assumptions into question, continue on to the next chapter. I'm going to describe two programs in some detail and recount the unexpected findings from my research with Joe Kahne that investigated what students actually learn. If you prefer to skip Chapter 7, you can flip right to Chapter 8, where I describe the characteristics of successful programs—lessons that colleagues and I have learned from a variety of initiatives that encourage students to practice democratic citizenship.

CHAPTER 7

Participatory and Social Justice– Oriented Citizens

Scholars who write about theories of democracy often blend commitments to participation with commitments to social justice. The political theorist Benjamin Barber, for example, wrote a popular and influential book called *Strong Democracy: Participatory Politics for a New Age*. In that book and much of his other writings, he focuses on forms of civic engagement that are specifically about democratic struggle and social justice.[1] Similarly, civic engagement scholar and founder of Public Achievement Harry Boyte advocates programs that engage young people in collective civic projects. Like Barber, Boyte frequently writes about historical examples of civic participation that embody the pursuit of social justice such as the example of those who worked in the civil rights campaigns of the 1950s and 1960s—men and women who participated in nonviolent actions of civil disobedience and whose work, it would be fair to say, exemplifies both participation and justice.[2] And it's not just theorists whose names start with the letter "B" either. Brilliant writers from turn-of-the-20th-century progressives Paul Hanna and William Kilpatrick to contemporary scholars Ira Shor, James Youniss, and Miranda Yates all call attention to the importance of both participation and the quest for social justice.[3] Educational programs built on these ideals follow the same thinking.

Combining these commitments makes a lot of sense: We want students who participate *and* think about the root causes of problems and ideals of justice. Developing commitments for both civic participation and social justice, as well as fostering the capacities to fulfill these commitments seems like a likely path toward a more democratic society. But studying actual on-the-ground programs, rather than just the theory, yields surprising results.[4]

> We want students who participate *and* think about the root causes of problems and ideals of justice.

Emphasizing both kinds of goals doesn't always result in the outcomes program leaders were hoping for. In fact, the evidence indicates that there is a difference between best intentions and actual program results. The theory and the practice don't always line up.

When on-the-ground practice fails to align with a given educational theory, theorists should take heed. When it comes to programs that aim to teach democratic citizenship, we should be wary of assuming that commitments to participatory citizenship and to justice necessarily align—because in practice, these two orientations resulted in different student outcomes. While pursuit of both goals may well support the development of a more democratic society, it is not clear whether making advances along one dimension will necessarily further progress on the other. Do programs that support civic participation necessarily promote students' capacities for critical analysis and social change? Conversely, when teachers focus on social justice, do they provide the foundation for effective and committed civic actors? Or might such programs support the development of armchair activists who have articulate conversations over coffee, without ever acting?

A number of programs teach students how government works and about how to get involved in community affairs (i.e., how to participate). Joe Kahne and I, along with a team of graduate students, studied some of these programs and their outcomes as part of an effort by a philanthropic foundation to boost civic engagement among young people through educational programming.[5] We also studied programs that aimed at more of a social justice–oriented approach. I'm going to draw on our writing about two of the programs we studied to illustrate the need to pay careful attention to each of these different kinds of goals. Both initiatives were designed to support the development of democratic and civic understandings and commitments in high school students. But the programs' goals and strategies differed. The first, which we call Madison County Youth Service League, aims to develop participatory citizens; the second, which we call Bayside Students for Justice, aims to develop social justice–oriented citizens. Although the focus here is on the differences between participatory and social justice–oriented visions of citizenship, you will see that personal responsibility plays a role in each of these programs as well. For readers interested in the technical details, the research I describe below has been published in academic journals, complete with charts and tables describing the statistical significance of the results.[6]

PARTICIPATORY CITIZENS:
THE MADISON COUNTY YOUTH SERVICE LEAGUE

The Madison County Youth Service League was located in a high school of a suburban/rural, largely middle-class East Coast community outside a city of roughly 23,000 people. The idea for the Youth Service League came to a social studies teacher after she had attended a speech by Benjamin Barber about the importance of engaging students in public life. A 20-year veteran, this teacher and a 2nd-year teacher taught a condensed and intensified version of a standard government course during the first semester of the academic year. For the second semester, they developed a service-learning curriculum: Students focused on particular topics related to their government curriculum as they worked in small teams on public service projects in their county's administrative offices. The goal, as one of the teachers explained, "is to produce kids that are active citizens in our community . . . kids that won't be afraid to go out and take part in their community . . . kids that understand that you have to have factual evidence to back up anything you say, anything you do."

One group of students investigated whether citizens in their community wanted curbside trash pickup that was organized by the county. Another group identified jobs that prisoners incarcerated for fewer than 90 days could perform and analyzed the cost of similar programs in other localities. Other students helped to develop a 5-year plan for the fire and rescue department. For each project, students had to collect and analyze data, interact with government agencies, write a report, and present their findings in a formal hearing before the county's Board of Supervisors.

The teachers of the Youth Service League believed that placing students in internships where they worked on meaningful projects under the supervision of committed role models would:

- Teach students how government worked
- Help students recognize the importance of being actively involved in community issues
- Provide students with the skills required for effective and informed civic involvement

When we surveyed and interviewed the students, we found plenty of evidence that the Madison County Youth Service League was very successful in achieving many of these goals.

Making Civic Education Meaningful

We observed the classroom and community-based activities, and we surveyed and interviewed students before and after they participated in the Youth Service League program. All the data indicated that the program had a significant impact on students, especially as it compared to traditional class work. Janine's reaction was typical:

> I learned more by doing this than I would just sitting in a classroom. . . . I mean, you really don't have hands-on activities in a classroom. But when you go out [to the public agencies] instead of getting to read about problems, we see the problems. Instead of, you know, writing down a solution, we make a solution.

Teresa, another student, said:

> I kind of felt like everything that we had been taught in class, how the whole government works. . . . We got to learn it and we got to go out and experience it. We saw things happening in front of us within the agency. I think it was more useful to put it together and see it happening instead of just reading from a book and learning from it.

Not only did the activities in the community help to enliven classroom learning, but many of the students' projects also tangibly affected the local community. Students often talked about the powerful impact of realizing that what they did would or could make a difference.

By engaging students in projects in the community, the Madison County Youth Service League had significant success making learning relevant to students, conveying practical knowledge about how to engage in community affairs, and demonstrating to students the ways in which classroom-based academic knowledge can be used for civic work in the community.

Making a Difference in the Lives of Others

The curriculum also developed students' desire to participate in civic affairs and gave them a sense that they can make a difference in the lives of others. When asked about how the program influenced their thinking, most students talked about how the experience deepened their belief in the importance of civic involvement. Emily, for example, spoke about the difference between talking about a problem and doing something active. In politics, she said, "The people always say their opinions and get mad about this and that but then they never do anything about what they feel." She went on to describe the ways her experience with the Youth Service League made her realize that "everyone needs to do their part if they want something to be done."

Students not only felt that they should be involved, but also that when they are involved, they are able get things done. In social science research, this is called a sense of civic efficacy. "We're just kids to most people," one student observed, "and I kind of figured that [grown-ups] wouldn't really give us the time of day." But through their participation in the Youth Service League, students learned that enough adults were "willing to help us."

Students also reported excitement at the prospect of getting involved in ways they did not know were available to them before their experience with the Youth Service League. One student talked about not having realized that towns and communities had "meetings all the time," adding that she thinks she'll be more likely to go to more community meetings when she's older. Another observed that if more people were aware of ways they could participate, "we wouldn't have as many problems, because they would understand that . . . people do have an impact."

The surveys we conducted before and after the students took the program, and the results of these surveys further illustrate many of these positive effects. The changes from before the students took the program to after were remarkable. Students expressed a greater belief that they had a personal responsibility to help others and that government should help those in need. The students evidenced a stronger sense that they could be effective leaders, an increased sense of confidence that they could make a difference in their communities, and a feeling of having a greater commitment to community involvement.

These results became even clearer the second year we studied the program, because the same two teachers taught both a Youth Service League class and another government class that did not participate in the Youth Service League curriculum. Students who had participated in the Service League curriculum again showed remarkable results on the measures described above, while students in the regular government class did not show changes on any of these measures.

A Vision of What to Do and the
Knowledge and Skills Needed to Do It

Youth Service League students also consistently spoke of the needs in their community and of their ideas about how to address these needs. For example, the group of students investigating curbside trash pickup conducted surveys of community residents, researched other communities' recycling programs, undertook a cost analysis, and examined charts of projected housing growth to estimate growth in trash and its cost and environmental implications. "We researched the Code of [Madison] County to find out . . . the legal requirements," one student explained. They met with county officials about their plan and wrote letters to the editors of local newspapers. Another group discovered that child immunization rates were low in their community and worked with the Health Department to develop ways to encourage parents to have their children immunized.

Another group learned how to analyze the tax code in order to survey community members about their tax preferences, phoning the Commissioner of Revenue's office when they needed information or explanations. Other groups wrote grants to raise money for student resources, or traveled to the state attorney's office to get information on crime rates in schools in order to develop a survey about crime for faculty and students.

Once again, the quantitative findings (surveys administered before and after their participation in the program) demonstrated that students gained confidence in their ability to help others and support community development. And the control group? Among the group of students in the regular government class, there were no significant changes in these measures.

A Summary of What Happened in
the Madison County Youth Service League

The Youth Service League aimed to promote civic participation consistent with a vision of participatory citizenship, to link service to academic content, and to provide a meaningful research experience. The program was highly successful in these areas. But the program did not aim to foster the justice-oriented citizen's understanding of structural or root causes of problems. While students did study controversial topics—such as requiring prisoners to work for small or no earnings or evaluating a detention center for juveniles—they did not consider structural issues or questions of systemic injustice. They did not examine data regarding the relationship among race, social class, and prison sentencing or question whether increased incarceration has lowered crime rates. They did not examine whether incarcerating juveniles (as opposed to other possible policies) increases or decreases the likelihood of future criminal activity or investigate which groups lobby for tougher or less-strict sentencing laws. Nor did they identify or discuss the diverse ideologies that inform political stances on such issues.

Consider also the project parameters of the group of students who examined their county's tax structure to identify possible ways to finance needed school construction. They conducted a survey to find out residents' preferences and found that 108 of 121 residents said no to the idea of a local income tax. These students did not discuss the reasons why so many residents oppose a local income tax or examine issues of equity when considering alternative options for taxation.

In general, we did not find evidence in student interviews, our observations, or our analysis of survey data that student projects and the associated analyses examined underlying political issues related to interest groups and the political process, the causes of poverty, different groups' access to health care, or the fairness of different systems of taxation (even though two projects focused on issues related to health care and taxation). Students focused on particular programs and policies and aimed for technocratic/value-neutral analysis.

Accordingly, our survey data did not indicate significant increases in measures related to justice-oriented citizenship. The program did not appear to alter students' interest in politics or political activity (e.g., voting, writing letters) or affect their commitment to work for justice. Nor did it alter their perspective on the degree to which structural rather than individual factors might contribute to poverty.

These findings are consistent with the stated goals of those who run the program. When asked to list characteristics of a "good citizen," program leaders cited qualities such as "honesty," "civic participation," "takes responsibility for others," "becomes involved in solving public problems," "active participant rather than passive," "educated about democracy, makes decisions based on facts," and "loyalty to God/country." To summarize, then, neither the goals of the teachers who developed and taught the Youth Service League curriculum nor the outcomes we measured included changes in students' interest in politics, their perspective on structural roots of social problems, or their commitment to social justice.

JUSTICE-ORIENTED CITIZENS:
BAYSIDE STUDENTS FOR JUSTICE

In the second program we studied, politics took center stage. Bayside Students for Justice is a curriculum developed as part of a social studies course in San Francisco's George Washington High School, which has a diverse student body. This program, inspired by the United Nations' Declaration of Human Rights, had goals oriented around improving society through structural changes. As one of the teachers put it, "My goal is to empower [students] to focus on things that they care about in their own lives and to . . . show them avenues that they can use to achieve real social change, profound social change." The program advanced a justice-oriented vision of citizenship which sought to teach students how to address structural issues of inequity and injustice and bring about social change. A program developer explained that:

> A good citizen actively organizes with other people [to address] causes of injustice and suffering. . . . A good citizen understands the complexities of social issues, political issues, and economic issues, and how they are tied together, and is not always willing to accept the definition of a problem as presented to them by politicians.

One group of students studied whether SAT exams are biased and created a pamphlet pointing out the weaknesses of the test in adequately predicting future student success in college. They distributed the pamphlet to the school and surrounding community.

Another group examined child labor practices worldwide and the social, political, and economic issues these practices raise. These students held schoolwide forums on their findings in an effort to inform students—many of whom wear the designer clothes and shoes manufactured by the corporations that the group investigated—of the child labor practices of these corporations. They also called on school officials to be aware of the labor practices employed by manufacturers from which the school purchased T-shirts and athletic uniforms. Jason's observation—typical of students interviewed about their experience—reflects the program's emphasis on justice: "It's amazing how all this exploitation is all around us and stuff; I mean we are even wearing clothes and we don't have [any] idea who makes them, how much they're paid, or where they work."

A third group investigated what they found to be a dearth of adequate education programs in juvenile detention centers, eventually making a video to publicize their findings. In a presentation to the school, this group reported that "Instead of buying books, they used money to put bars on windows [that] don't even open." "We wanted to show that not all the kids in there are that bad," one of the students said. "If our youth is the future of our country, then we'd better take care of [them] even if they're in trouble."

The teachers of the Bayside Students for Justice program believed that having students seek out and address areas of injustice in society would:

- Sensitize students to the diverse needs and perspectives of fellow citizens
- Teach students to recognize injustice and critically assess root causes of social problems
- Provide students with an understanding of how to change established systems and structures

Bayside Students for Justice, like Madison County, was successful in meeting many of the curriculum planners' stated goals. Bayside students, for example, also noted the importance of making their classroom learning meaningful. One class member reported that "I don't like to learn just by reading because it goes in one ear and out the other; but in this class we can really make a difference." Others noted: "This class was more exciting because it was more real," "We were out there instead of just with our heads in the books," and "I liked feeling like we could do something positive." Ayisha spoke about the connection in this way: "Before this experience, I thought school was just about passing this test or that test. . . . Now I finally see [that] you can use your knowledge of history to make a better world." Also, like their Madison County counterparts, Bayside students indicated an increased sense of civic efficacy (the

> "Before this experience, I thought school was just about passing this test or that test. . . . Now I finally see [that] you can use your knowledge of history to make a better world."

confidence that if they try, they can get something done), likely owing to their experiences in the community and an increased belief that government had a responsibility to help those in need.

But while the Bayside and Madison County curricular experiences shared a number of features, other aspects of the curriculum, the goals, and the impact on students differed significantly. For example, survey results from Bayside reflected the program's emphasis on critical social analysis and on understanding underlying forces that affect social policy. Students demonstrated greater ability to consider structural explanations for poverty and greater interest in politics and political issues overall—areas in which Youth Service League students showed no change. Conversely, Bayside students did not demonstrate gains in their knowledge about particular community groups or about the technical challenges and possibilities that were associated with particular policies and initiatives, while the Youth Service League students showed evidence of progress in these areas. Students who participated in the Madison County Youth Service League improved their leadership skills, vision, and knowledge related to civic participation (as well as their sense of personal responsibility to help others), while Bayside students did not.

Our study of Bayside helps us understand the reasons for these different outcomes. At the center of Bayside's approach were commitments to critical and structural social analysis, to making the personal political, and to collective responsibility for action.

Critical and Structural Social Analysis

The class that best illustrates Bayside Students for Justice's focus on critical analysis and social critique was led by Terri Camajani, a veteran social studies teacher and one of the founders of Bayside Students for Justice. Camajani sees an understanding of social justice as an essential component of informed citizenship. Adorning her classroom walls are several posters with quotations from well-known educators, religious leaders, and social critics. Those featured include Bishop Dom Helder Camara, "When I give food to the poor, they call me a saint. When I ask why the poor have no food, they call me a communist," and Paulo Freire, "Washing one's hands of the conflict between the powerful and the powerless means to side with the powerful, not to be neutral."

Camajani had her students study a variety of manifestations of violence in their community, including domestic violence, child abuse, and gang violence. They arrived at this choice through a process in which the teacher had them "map" their communities (to gain a sense of what issues affected their own lives and the lives of others) and write about an issue that deeply angered or affected them. Using a weighted vote, students came up with violence as an issue they found both common across their lives and deplorable in its social consequences. Their work on this topic was combined with a curriculum on domestic violence prevention.

In class, they focused on the causes and consequences of violence in their lives and in their community. They began by sharing stories of their own experiences with violence (at home, in their neighborhood, and at school). One student, for example, talked about a shooting incident she had witnessed several blocks from her house. Another wrote about his experience with domestic violence in his family. What made this teacher's approach relatively unique, however, was not the focus on violence; many teachers discuss violence with students in urban classrooms. In fact, violence-prevention lessons are often part of programs that might easily be characterized as developing personally responsible citizens rather than justice-oriented citizens (see below). What made the approach unique was the way this teacher engaged students in a discussion of the social and economic forces that contribute to violence.

In one classroom activity, students compared demographic data on per capita income broken down by neighborhood with data on the prevalence of violent crime, also broken down by neighborhood. Students also explored different beliefs about violence expressed by politicians, writers, the media, and community groups and organizations. At virtually every stage of the curriculum, their own stories and incidents of violence reported in the media were examined in relation to broader social, political, and economic forces. Students used their own and their classmates' experiences as a means for exploring ways to prevent violence and promote human rights and social justice. In another class session, for example, Camajani asked, "What does violence reveal about what else is going on and how can we fix it?" The class then created a reverse flowchart, starting at the bottom where an incident of domestic violence had occurred and connecting it to events and forces that might have provoked the violence. One student, Tameka, posited, "There must have been a lot of tension in the house." The following exchange ensued:

Teacher: And what might have led to that much tension?
Keri: Maybe Dad lost his job.
Hector: And then he started drinking.
Keri: Maybe there's no money.
Teacher: We can't really know, right, but there could be a lot of
   pressure on these people right now.

Through this and similar discussions, students focused their thinking on relationships between structural dynamics and the behavior of individuals. A number of classroom discussions also focused on the differences between legislative or political approaches to social problems other than violence (e.g., environmental regulations) and those focused on individual, voluntary behavior, or "character."

Making the Personal Political

At the same time that structural dynamics were examined in relation to individual behavior, personal responsibility also received substantial attention. For example, some of the violence-prevention activities in which the students participated taught students to control their anger and stressed the need to always consider the consequences of their actions. Many character traits of a personally responsible citizen are important to Bayside's enactment of the justice-oriented citizen.

However, unlike many other programs that emphasize personal responsibility (like the character-education programs I described in Chapter 5), Bayside's approach did not merely exhort students to adopt certain values or behaviors such as self-control, honesty, punctuality, and caring for others; it also included an implicit critique of the way society is structured and encouraged students to examine the relationship between those structures and the way individuals behave. Approaches like those used by Camajani challenge the exclusive focus on personal responsibility without rejecting the basic premise that the ways in which children and adults behave is important. These approaches conclude that an individual's character does matter, but that character can best be understood—and changed—through social analysis and attention to root causes of social injustices. The program seeks to enhance students' understanding of society rather than simply giving students a list of values they are to embrace and behaviors they are magically supposed to adopt.

In Camajani's class, students discussed social, political, and economic factors that reinforce notions that men are superior to women and that they should enforce that superiority if it is challenged. As a result, some men turn violent, and some women learn to tolerate their violence. Thus, in addition to talking about how to take greater responsibility for improving their own behavior with respect to violence and anger, students talked about their own experiences with violence in order to better understand and develop strategies to change institutions, structures, or conditions that cause or encourage violent behavior.

Contrasting this curricular approach with the Character Counts! Coalition's take on how to avoid violence (recall that Character Counts! falls squarely into the category of a program that wants to teach students to be personally responsible), it becomes clear the ways Bayside Students for Justice incorporates important aspects of the personally responsible citizen into its emphasis on both understanding unjust social contexts and pursuing just ones. The Character Counts! coalition advocates respect, good manners, dealing peacefully with anger, and so on. Camajani points out the importance of some of these lessons at the same time that she makes clear its limitations. For example, she and her students discuss whether individual responsibility is enough to end racism or sexism or poverty or whether individual responsibility needs to be combined with efforts to address the causes of these conditions "farther up the river."

If there is a lesson to be learned about personal responsibility for Camajani, it is that personal experiences and behavior both result from and are indicators of broader social and economic conditions. For Bayside Students for Justice, personal responsibility requires that people study and seek to change these conditions. With this recognition, Camajani is able to structure a curriculum that promotes citizens who are both personally responsible and justice oriented, something few programs are able to achieve.

Collective Responsibility for Action

Not only do students learn about the ways in which individual behavior often results from societal factors; they also learn that social change is the product of collective effort. Even before students started the research and service aspects of their projects, their teacher noted that, through the process of community mapping and choosing their topic, students had begun to think of themselves differently. They had begun to see themselves as part of a youth community with the potential to transform and improve society in positive ways.

In interviews and written assignments for class, students demonstrated their understanding of a collective rather than individual vision for making change. After listening in class to the song "We Who Believe in Freedom" by Sweet Honey in the Rock, one young man wrote that "whether the struggle is big or small it should be everyone's responsibility together. . . . Movements are not about me, they're about us." Another student—a football player—observed that there's "a lot of camaraderie on the field, but in the classroom, it seems like everyone works as an individual to better themselves. In this class, we're working as a group to better everything around us."

Thus, in contrast to programs that seek to teach that "one person can make a difference," Bayside Students for Justice emphasized the importance (and effectiveness) of addressing social problems collectively.

THE IMPORTANCE OF RECOGNIZING DIFFERENT CONCEPTIONS OF CITIZENSHIP

Did the Madison County Youth Service League do a better job than Bayside Students for Justice at educating citizens, or was Bayside more effective? That's up to you to decide. My goal here is to make clear that different democratic values are embedded in these efforts. Both programs were effective at achieving goals that were consistent with their respective underlying conceptions of citizenship. Yet the research on these programs demonstrates important differences in impact. The Youth Public Service League appeared to have a powerful impact on students' capacities for and commitments to civic participation. Students could detail the skills they used (e.g., conducting polls, interviewing officials, making presentations, reading legislation), as well as the knowledge they gained about how government works. Survey measures of students' sense of personal responsibility to help others, their vision of how to help, and their leadership efficacy showed significant improvements. Especially notable from both our surveys and interviews was the change in students' confidence that they had the knowledge or "social capital" to make things happen in the community. Interviews, observations, and examples of student work all reinforced the survey finding of a dramatic increase in students' sense that they had knowledge of what resources were available to help with community projects and of how to contact and work effectively with community organizations to mobilize those resources. This confidence grew out of their involvement in substantive projects that required frequent interaction with multiple community actors and agencies.

Madison County students also spoke extensively during interviews about the micro-politics and technical challenges associated with their projects. "I thought there was cooperation amongst the departments," one Madison student told us, "but then the more we got into it the more I realized Person One is in charge of A, B, and C and Person Two is in charge of X, Y, and Z." Students were frustrated that various departments did not work well together and with what they identified as "turf issues." Many noted a poor working relationship between the county and the city.

We did not, however, see evidence that the Youth Service League program sparked interest in or conveyed knowledge of broad social critiques and systemic reform. Madison students tended to downplay or ignore explicitly political or ideologically contentious issues. They were not able to talk about how varied interests and power relationships or issues of race and social class might be related to the lack of consensus on priorities and the inability of these varied groups to work together effectively. Since these kinds of issues were not discussed as part of the curriculum, it is not surprising that students did not end up demonstrating much interest in or knowledge about the structural and individual causes of poverty. Nor did their interest in talking about or being involved in politics change.

To a much greater degree, Bayside's students talked about the need for forms of civic involvement that addressed issues of social justice and systemic inequities that might be altered. When asked whether violence prevention programs that focus on individual behavior could eliminate domestic violence, one student, Desiree, both praised those kinds of programs and noted the importance of broader analysis. She said, "We saw a lot of examples of people who are trying to do their best, but are still being brought down" by forces that are bigger than the individual. Other students talked about the complexity of intractable social problems like poverty or racism. After telling the class about his cousin who was arrested for carrying a weapon, Derrick wondered aloud to the class about the connection among unemployment, anger, desperation, and violence, asking whether people in the class thought

it would work to just "teach everyone to be good." Tamika put it this
way: "Lots of people want to be nice,
[but] if you don't got food for your
kids, how nice is that?"

> "Lots of people want to be nice,
> [but] if you don't got food for
> your kids, how nice is that?"

Compared with students from Madison County, students who
took part in the Bayside Students for Justice curriculum appeared to
emphasize social critique significantly more and technocratic skills
associated with participation somewhat less. For example, students
were more likely at the end of the program than at the beginning to
posit structural explanations for social problems (stating, for example,
that the problem of poverty resulted from too few jobs that pay wages
that are high enough to support a family, rather than being a result
of individuals being lazy and not wanting to work). They were more
likely than their Madison County peers to be interested in and want to
discuss politics and political issues, and they were more likely to seek
redress of root causes of difficult social ills. As one student told us after
several months in the Bayside program, "When the economy's bad
and people start blaming immigrants or whoever else they can blame,
they've got to realize that there are big social, economic, and political
issues tied together, that it's not the immigrants, no, it's bigger than
them."

To the extent that Bayside students learned about participatory
skills, they focused on extra-governmental social activism that challenged rather than reinforced existing norms (such as community
organizing or protesting). Evidence from observations, interviews,
student work, and surveys of Bayside's students did not show an increase in students' knowledge about particular community resources.
Unlike their Madison County peers, Bayside students' sense that they
were effective community leaders (e.g., knowing how to run meetings) remained unchanged. Nor was there any increase in students'
personal responsibility to help others (as opposed to their inclination
for collective action for change that was frequently expressed during
interviews).

Programs that successfully educate for democracy can promote
very different outcomes. Some programs may foster the ability or the
commitment to participate while others may prompt critical analysis
that focuses on macro structural issues, the role of interest groups,
power dynamics, and/or social justice. And these differences often
are important. Answering the question "Which program better de-
velops citizens?" necessarily engages the politics that surround varied

conceptions of citizenship because it begs a definition of a better citizen. Those who view civic participation as of primary importance would likely view the Madison County Youth Service League program as extraordinarily effective.

However, those who believe that students should learn how to examine social structures and deliberate principles and practices of justice might well be troubled that participants in the Madison County program did not talk about the need for structural change, about methods used historically to bring change about (e.g., those employed by various social movements), or about social injustice. Educators who wish to teach students to support social change might therefore value the explicit attention and critiques that students participating in Bayside Students for Justice developed. Bayside students learned about ways in which the interests of powerful groups are often supported by institutions and social structures. They also expanded their interest in following broader local and national political issues.

THE INFLUENCE OF COMMUNITY CONTEXT

The social context and political norms of a given community influence local curricular decisions as well as the impact of curriculum on students. Bayside and Madison County, for example, are very different communities. It may well be that Bayside's urban school environment exposed students to more forms of injustice and rhetoric related to injustice than Madison County students encountered in their largely homogeneous middle-class community. This exposure, in turn, may have made it more likely that Bayside students would gravitate toward justice-oriented themes than students from Madison County.

From responses on our pre-surveys, we know that youth in the two communities started off in different places on several relevant measures. Bayside students were far more likely to offer structural explanations for poverty than were Madison County youth, and Madison County youth were much more likely to express confidence in their knowledge related to community development. What's particularly interesting about our post-survey results is that they demonstrate that on top of these initial differences, Bayside's curriculum led students to support structural explanations even more strongly, and Madison County's curriculum led students to hold even greater confidence in their knowledge related to community development.

The differing political climates certainly influenced teacher's options. This was evident, for example, in the reaction of the Youth Service League director to the social critique focus of Bayside Students for Justice and other groups (who met three times during our study to discuss their programs with each other). She told us: "If my superintendent or board heard me saying what you all are saying, I'd be fired." When it comes to politically contentious topics, context matters. The ways in which contexts shape both the constraints placed on teachers and the curriculum's impact on students clearly deserves extensive study.

PURSUING DUAL GOALS

Those committed to educating toward justice-oriented citizenship would ideally want to couple critical analysis of root causes of injustice with opportunities to develop capac-

> Engaging in critical analysis does not necessarily foster the ability or the commitment to participate.

ities for participation. They want students to be able both to analyze and to understand structural causes of deeply entrenched social problems and gain the skills and motivation to act by participating in local and national politics and community forums. But a focus on justice guarantees neither the motivation nor the capacity to participate in democratic change. Many would applaud programs that manage to emphasize justice-oriented citizenship linked to a desire and capacity for participation. However, our research indicates that engaging in critical analysis does not necessarily foster the ability or the commitment to participate. The reverse is also true: Students can learn to participate without engaging in critical analysis that focuses on macrostructural issues, the role of interest groups, power dynamics, and/or social justice. The ability to spot injustice is not organically linked to the inclination or the ability to take action.[7]

Yet there are programs that serve as important examples for the kind of engaged and purposeful teaching and learning that strengthens democratic societies. In the following chapter, I describe several programs that proved successful in just those ways. They combine personal responsibility, participation, and an orientation toward social justice in ways that make teaching and learning meaningful and are also supportive of democratic civic goals.

CHAPTER 8

Thinking, Engaged Citizens

I know I can't save the whole world, but when I see something go wrong, I need to say something. I just can't keep my mouth shut, because this experience has changed me.

—Stephanie, The Overground Railroad

There are many varied and powerful ways to teach children and young adults to think in ways that promote civic engagement with important issues. In Chapter 7, I described two distinct programs (the Madison County Youth Service League and Bayside Students for Justice) that were part of a larger study Joe Kahne and I undertook of initiatives that put civic engagement at the center of their efforts. Since that study, both independently and together, we have worked with teams of graduate students and colleagues to continue exploring a variety of school- and community-based approaches. We studied 10th-graders evaluating a juvenile detention center, 9th-graders studying the feasibility of curbside recycling, and 11th-graders reporting to the public on the availability of affordable housing in their community. We examined programs that exposed university students to community-development projects in Silicon Valley, or that brought theology majors to a reservation to study the history of Native American experience. We visited an education program with a 70-year history of working for social and economic change through education and democratic action. Many of these programs show impressive effects on students' abilities to connect what they are learning to social and civic goals.[1]

In this chapter, I describe a few of these programs. Although all of these approaches to teaching democratic engagement differ in structure, organization, and goals, each incorporates characteristics of the personally responsible, the participatory, and the social justice–oriented citizen in unique ways. Some are implemented within a single subject-area course, others are whole-school initiatives, and still others are even broader programs that are available nationally. But they do share some characteristics. They are all inspiring. They all give teachers the freedom and flexibility to design curriculum in ways that take advantage of local contexts—that is, they are not standardized. They are all built on the assumption that students are highly capable, able to rise to the challenges that are presented. Each program requires students to engage critically with real-life issues in thoughtful ways. Each one consciously links learning to the preparation of thoughtful, active, and democratically engaged citizens.

CONNECTING LEARNING TO SOCIAL AND CIVIC GOALS

"Why do we have to know this?" "Is this going to be on the test?" These are two of the many questions teachers commonly hear that highlight what students often perceive as the disconnect between what goes on in classrooms and the social, political, and economic life outside of them. At the same time, most of us have had rich learning experiences that tie academic knowledge and skills to relevant individual and community interests. Those experiences, however, are too often isolated or episodic rather than central to the learning experience. The programs below showcase approaches that connect school and community, and which connect learning to social and civic goals.

El Puente Academy

El Puente Academy in the Williamsburg neighborhood of Brooklyn, New York, ties the entire school curriculum to students' and teachers' concerns about the community. Founded by and situated within the El Puente community center and named a New York City School of Excellence, El Puente boasts a 90% graduation rate in an area where schools usually see only 50% of their students graduate in 4 years. Former El Puente principal Héctor Calderón attributes the school's success to a curriculum that engages students in community efforts to reverse cycles of poverty and violence and work toward change in their own neighborhood. Students study environmental hazards in the area, not only because they care about the health of the natural environment, but also because these hazards directly affect the health of the community to which they are deeply committed. Classroom activities are designed to cover basic skills, but also to integrate those

> At El Puente, fifty 10th- and 11th-grade students surveyed the community to chart levels of asthma and identify families affected by the disease. The students' report became the first by a community organization to be published in a medical journal.

skills into meaningful projects that show students the connections between their academic learning and community engagement.[2]

In one curriculum unit at El Puente, fifty 10th- and 11th-grade students surveyed the community to chart levels of asthma and identify families affected by the disease. In preparation for the survey, the math teacher devoted a curriculum unit to the use (and misuse) of statistics and the English teacher assigned literature dealing with themes of urban poverty. In science, students learned about epidemiology and the ways in which doctors and scientists track diseases; and in social studies, students explored issues related to economic inequality and health. Students and teachers also worked closely with an organization (Community Information and Epidemiological Technologies) that helps communities conduct audits of a variety of health-related public services, providing surveying techniques and other advice that supplemented the work students were doing in their subject-area classes. The students' report, which linked elevated asthma levels in the neighborhood to automobile traffic and nearby factories, became the first by a community organization to be published in a medical journal.

Students and teachers also employed concepts of responsibility, participation, and justice when they helped wage a successful community outreach campaign to prevent a 15-story incinerator from being built in their neighborhood. Teachers used the campaign as an opportunity to teach the importance of taking both personal and collective responsibility for community issues, and they highlighted connections to issues of social justice that infused the school curriculum. This effort garnered national attention when, together with the El Puente Community Center, youth and adults alike worked across historic divisions between Hispanic community residents who live on the south side of Williamsburg and Hasidic Jews who live on the north side. "We all breathe the same air," observed Luis Garden Acosta, founder and president of the community center.[3]

In another project, senior students identified six abandoned properties in Williamsburg and neighboring Bushwick. After selecting one of these properties for its potential value to the community, the students wrote reports that proposed recommendations for its development. Incorporating information on such topics as unfair lending practices and the problems of gentrification, each report included a scale drawing of the site, a development budget for the site, a financial plan for acquiring and developing the site, and a proposal for how the site should be developed. Once again, subject-area teachers mobilized their disciplines in the service of social and civic goals, linking core academic content goals to broader issues of social and communal concern. After completing assignments that helped to develop students' cognitive skills in a variety of related ways, the students prepared recommendations to present to the Community Board.[4] Students gained knowledge about loans, interest rates, architecture, and design. They also discovered how to make a difference in their community by converting abandoned buildings into usable space.[5]

El Puente students learn that thinking requires research, analysis, and interpretation—all of which are difficult to learn from an exclusive focus on narrow tests of knowledge and skills when divorced from social, political, and economic contexts.[6] Moreover, the curricular lessons at El Puente reinforce the vital role played by teachers in conveying to students that what they think and do matters. In his book *Experience and Education*, John Dewey described the role of the teacher in similar terms. "The educator," he wrote, "is responsible for [selecting activities] which lend themselves to social organization, an organization in which all individuals have an opportunity to contribute something.[7] Teaching that engages students' interests, talents, and abilities in the service of improving their neighborhood and the broader community results in educational programs that connect learning to meaningful community engagement. Engaging students in authentic ways is at the heart of El Puente's mission.

Project V.O.I.C.E./Spanish 511

In Phillips Academy, a residential independent school in Andover, Massachusetts, Project V.O.I.C.E. (Vote on Inner City Empowerment)/ Spanish 511 integrates language study and the community.[8] The program brings high school students in a Spanish language class together with Hispanic adults in the neighboring city of Lawrence who are studying for their U.S. citizenship exam. The Spanish students experience intensive Spanish speaking as they and the adults discuss their ideas about citizenship and the value of democratic participation. The students also gain direct experience with the Hispanic immigrant community in Lawrence and an awareness of Hispanic immigrants in the rest of the country. Adults from the community of Lawrence, in turn, gain an opportunity to study one-on-one for their citizenship exam as well as practice their English while meeting and getting to know the Phillips Academy students.

When I first studied this program, it had just begun as a collaboration between Becky McCann, the Spanish teacher, and Chad Green, the community service coordinator for Phillips Academy.[9] Free from the restrictions now faced by too many teachers in developing unique and exciting curriculum, they were able to build on an interdisciplinary goal they felt passionate about: to use language study to bridge the socioeconomic divide between wealthier Andover and economically depressed Lawrence. They also hoped to familiarize students with a range of issues related to democracy and social justice, bringing together concerns about individual responsibility, collective action, and social justice at the same time as their students developed their Spanish language skills.[10] With the help of the Lawrence Family Development and Education Fund (LFDEF), the course they created sought to encourage active civic participation among both the students and the Lawrence community adults.

The classes met four times each week—with one session each week in Lawrence. Occasional guests, films, and projects peppered the curriculum. For example, the students prepared extensive materials to aid the Hispanic adults in their preparation for the citizenship exam, including videos, audios, and notebook guides. Because some of the adults could not read in any language, the students assembled pictures of politicians, historical figures, the White House, and various American historical symbols to assist in their teaching. At the beginning and end of the course, students were also asked to write about what they thought constitutes good citizenship, and they participated in a simulation activity designed to encourage students to examine who holds power in any particular society and/or class and "how that power is obtained and maintained."

Since Lawrence—site of the famous Bread and Roses strike of 1912—had high levels of poverty in comparison to its nearby communities, the students prepared for their time in the community by reading articles about the economic and social context of the city and surrounding areas. The students then participated in a structured tour of Lawrence that included learning about key landmarks and neighborhoods and the history of the Lawrence textile mills, factories, and housing projects. The students also attended a panel discussion on low-income housing in Lawrence (conducted in Spanish) that took place in the Lawrence community center, and posed prepared questions to the moderators. The panelists included a mix of community-engaged professionals and volunteers, some of whom worked in Lawrence and some of whom both worked and lived there. The tour of Lawrence, the panel discussion, and article assignments and class discussions all helped to focus students' attention on the democratic implications of legislation, common stereotypes, economic divisions, and social stratification.

It would be difficult to overstate the value of the community work in which these students were engaged. Indeed, nearly all students, when asked how they might change the course, noted that "it should be a year long so we have more time in Lawrence" and "we should go to Lawrence twice each week for better continuity and more contact." This not only speaks well to the perceived value of the experience but also to the creative bridging of language instruction with community-engagement goals.

The primary goal for a high-level Spanish course is of course to learn Spanish. McCann, the instructor for the course, told us that "as a language teacher, I'm looking for an opportunity for our students to connect what they've learned in the classroom to authentic situations outside of the classroom." The class appears highly effective at motivating students in speaking, writing, and practicing conversational Spanish. On-the-ground opportunities to speak Spanish also resulted in a tendency to see the social utility of knowing a foreign language. For example, one student reported that the course was the most enjoyable language course she had taken. "This class," she said, "takes Spanish off the page, and it is incredibly gratifying to be able to go and communicate with someone from such a completely different background."

In addition to the opportunity to speak continuous Spanish for 45 minutes in a "real-life" setting with the Andover adults, students also emphasized both the hands-on and consequential nature of this kind of learning. Many students noted that they took this course as an alternative to the Spanish literature course (to continue in upper-level Spanish courses, they need to choose one or the other) because they, for example, "really enjoy working with people and knowing that I am making a difference in someone else's life and I'm not just sitting in a classroom trying to get a grade." Going to Lawrence, noted another student, "is the highlight of the week."

Other students reflected on their own or other students' changing perceptions of people who are different from themselves:

> These people are immigrants. I cringe when I think about how, before taking this course, I used to think the word sounds dirty or something.

> Learning firsthand about some of the experiences of the immigrants here in Lawrence reflects on other places like Washington Heights in New York where there is a huge Dominican population. And not just Hispanics, because all immigrants share some similar experiences, whether it's Asian or African or European. They face the same kinds of problems finding jobs and facing racism.

Another student talked about the impact the program had on her thinking about democratic rights and responsibilities:

> I can't take anything for granted anymore, because he will say, "you can vote" and go on about all these benefits I get because I'm a citizen. I was born here so it just came with the package. I didn't ask for it. I can vote in the next presidential elections and he can't vote—only if he passes his test.

Class discussions, the tour of Lawrence, and the panel on immigrants to which I referred above seem to have reinforced the structural concerns of democracy and justice as well as modeled the importance and processes of democratic debate. Panelists, for example, spoke (in Spanish) about the high incidence of lead paint in houses in Lawrence, cycles of poverty, and inadequate services.

For several students, the experience they had in Lawrence and with meeting panelists seems to have spurred thinking about possible career choices:

> I learned more in that hour panel than I have in this term's course material or readings—and we had really good articles to read. But what you get by speaking to somebody who's been through it versus just reading something about somebody is a

real sense of the issues. . . . I really hope that I'll be able to find a position someday in life where I can do the exact same thing they do.

Working across two distinct economic and cultural demographic locations brought together concerns about individual responsibility, collective participation and action, and social justice in an organic way, organized around developing Spanish language skills, and it accomplished these goals while instilling in students an intrinsic desire for community engagement. The collaboration also succeeded in building relationships between the Academy students and the Lawrence community adults. This special arrangement—in which the students are learning Spanish and the adults are studying for their citizenship exam—creates unique opportunities for authentic interactions that are less fraught with noblesse oblige than other service experiences. Students observed that "at the same time they are getting a view into our culture, we are getting a view into theirs." Another noted that "while we're trying to learn their language, they're also trying to learn English, so we're kind of putting both of them together at the same time."

Project V.O.I.C.E./Spanish 511 engages students and teachers in a collective, local project in the community. It encourages students to think critically about social, political, and economic conditions in both Andover and Lawrence. And it holds high expectations that students can take actions that make a difference—not only to the lives of the residents of Lawrence—but also to their own.

The Overground Railroad

A number of programs we studied seek to develop personal responsibility, community participation, and the ability to think critically by connecting contemporary community issues to past struggles. Historical examples of social movements can serve as reminders of the responsibilities of participation and the possibilities for change. The Overground Railroad is one such program. It brings together college students and faculty members from six colleges over the summer to learn in intensive and experiential ways about the civil rights movement of the 1960s and its implications for citizenship today.[11] It creates opportunities for students that showcase public works and possibilities for careers in community engagement.

For 3 weeks, students in the Overground Railroad project travel throughout the South, visiting historic sites of the antislavery and civil rights movements and meeting with key actors in the latter movement. They watch films about civil rights—such as the PBS documentary series *Eyes on the Prize*—read related academic literature, and discuss and analyze their experiences during daily seminars. When they return to their respective campuses in the fall, they initiate service projects that are informed by the ideas and strategies they studied. The students receive college credit through their participation.

The summer we studied the Overground Railroad, Dorothy Cotton, a leader in the civil rights movement, co-led much of the trip, and students met with an impressive array of civil rights leaders, community organizers, and lawyers. In Birmingham, Alabama, they met with leaders of the freedom movement at the Civil Rights Institute. They spoke with Reverend Fred Shuttlesworth, a cofounder of the Southern Christian Leadership Conference, about events in Birmingham in the 1960s and his role in the broader civil rights movement. They traveled to Selma, Alabama, to meet a woman who had been part of the famous civil rights march across the Edmund Pettus Bridge in 1965. In Memphis, Tennessee, they talked with one of the Black sanitation workers who had conducted a strike in 1968, and with Judge Sugarman, then a lawyer working on the sanitation workers' case. Other stops on their trip included numerous museums and the Highlander Folk School in New Market, Tennessee, where they discussed, among other issues, the role of music in social and political history.

On one of the Overground Railroad "stops," the students viewed a presentation by Reverend Teresa Jones, who recalled personal experiences of intimidation and violence during the early 1960s when she was helping to register Black voters in southern counties. Subsequent interviews with and surveys of participants in the Overground Railroad indicated that students drew substantial strength from these kinds of encounters—strength that helped them imagine choices that often conflicted with the norms and priorities of their peers. One student recognized that when Reverend Jones helped to organize the voter registration drive, she was not much older than he was now. This student observed that those "teenagers were . . . willing to put their lives on the line so that I could sit here and hold a conversation with you."

When students returned to their campuses the following fall, their service projects took varied forms. Some worked with elementary, middle, and high school students on educational projects about the civil rights movement. Others took part in presentations, speaking to and working with school and community groups, and designed lessons suited to various ages and levels of expertise as a means of sharing their newly acquired knowledge and experience. These service initiatives required students to draw on and synthesize what they had learned and to think about ways they could communicate their thoughts and knowledge effectively. This new knowledge presented opportunities for historical understanding as well as engagement with contemporary issues of concern. But for some students, the experience also led to expanded notions of future community engagement. One student, reflecting on what she learned, told us, "When I speak about these issues I can speak with more conviction. . . . The things that I have learned in this program have changed me."

The Overground Railroad project was also notable for the ways it expanded students' sense of their career possibilities. When Reverend Jones ended her presentation about what happened in the 1960s, she added, "That's what we did when we were in college . . . now it's your turn." Her message was clear: Her stories were not to be dismissed as titillating tidbits of a nostalgic past but rather stories about what is possible when citizens commit to act. The program used connection to the past to show students the possibilities for the future, that ordinary people can work together to improve society and achieve extraordinary results. "Now it's your turn" was an appeal these students took seriously.

SCALING UP:
REGIONAL AND NATIONAL PROGRAMS

In addition to these individual school and community group–based programs described in the previous section, other organized initiatives toward democratic engagement span an entire city, a state, or even the whole country. They demonstrate the untapped potential for democratically engaged teaching and learning that encourages meaningful thinking. Like the individual examples mentioned above, broad programs such as Public Achievement, the Mikva Challenge, and Earthforce share an emphasis on helping students to identify and act on issues of importance to themselves and to society and thus enable them to experience a sense of meaningful learning in the process.[12] Similarly, the Constitutional Rights Foundation's CityWorks curriculum is another

"scaled-up" program that effectively combines aspects of personal responsibility, political participation, and social justice.[13]

Expanding these programs locally or nationally, however, does
not mean they are cookie cutter. In all of these programs, teachers
and other local educators are expected to make local decisions based
on their own experiences in their local context. This stands in sharp
contrast to state or national curriculum dictates that mandate compliance with particular content or procedures. Two programs serve as
examples of "scaled-up" programs that work.

Generation Citizen, founded in 2009 by two students at Brown
University in Providence, Rhode Island, and now with offices in three
cities (Providence, New York, and San Francisco), offers some 6,000
high school and college students opportunities to learn about and
practice civic skills such as organizing petitions and letter-writing
campaigns, writing opinion pieces for newspapers, and convening
community meetings.[14] Generation Citizen works with middle school
and high school teachers, providing them with lesson plans and sup-
plementary materials not only to discuss, but which are also designed
to demonstrate the importance of democratic practices. Students, as
one teacher-adopter of the program explains, "are more than just
future workers. We also need to empower our students to care about
their community and become active citizens so that we can create a
community worth working in."[15]

While Generation Citizen still has room to expand geographically,
the Center for Civic Education's "We the People" program is active in
all 50 states, partnering with a variety of state bar associations, colleges
and universities, and civic and nonprofit organizations to foster teaching and learning about the Constitution and Bill of Rights. Providing
curricular materials (i.e., textbooks and lesson plans) and professional
development to elementary and secondary teachers interested in pro-
moting civic competencies and democratic ideals,[16] the program also
offers an online Constitution course where teachers and students can
explore topics such as the historical foundations of the American political system and the roles of citizens in American democracy.[17]

SCALING DOWN: THINKING ABOUT A THINKING CURRICULUM

As much as policymakers love the idea of programs with infinitely
broad impact, teaching primarily happens between a teacher and a

small group of individuals at a particular time and place. Although national initiatives can be helpful in structuring local efforts, in the end it is teachers who should be both expected and encouraged to pursue projects that draw on their own and their students' interests and capabilities. A flexible curriculum that emphasizes robust thinking about the role of citizens in democratic societies can take many forms. However, common characteristics can be seen in many teachers' efforts.

For example, Bob Peterson, a one-time Wisconsin Elementary Teacher of the Year, worked with his students at La Escuela Fratney in Milwaukee to examine the full spectrum of ideological positions that emerged following the September 11, 2001, terrorist attacks. Instead of avoiding the challenging questions posed by his 5th-grade students, Peterson encouraged them, placing a notebook prominently at the front of the classroom labeled "Questions That We Have." As the students discussed their questions and the unfolding current events, Peterson repeatedly asked students to consider their responsibilities to one another, to their communities, and to the world. Through poetry (Langston Hughes's "Let America Be America Again"); historical readings (the Declaration of Independence, the U.S. Constitution, the 1918 Sedition Act); and current events (photographs of September 11 memorial gatherings, protests in the United States and abroad, newspaper editorials), Peterson allowed students to explore political events surrounding the September 11 attacks and their effect on American patriotism and democracy.[18]

Similarly, longtime teacher Brian Schultz's inspiring efforts with his 5th-grade class in Chicago's Cabrini-Green housing project area included having his students conduct research on improving conditions in their own neighborhood, especially with regard to broken promises to build a new school. His students studied historical approaches to change and, rejecting passivity, demonstrated a deep attachment to their community and their neighbors. Their research on urban poverty in Chicago also led them to consider multiple perspectives on its causes, consequences, and possible solutions. Schultz, now a professor at Northeastern Illinois University in Chicago, describes these in his 2008 book, *Spectacular Things Happen Along the Way*.[19] Schultz developed his curriculum without a regional or national program overseeing his efforts, but his teaching approaches benefited from exposure to other educators who were engaged in similar work. His students not only examined root causes of problems but also participated in community efforts to ameliorate those problems. In the process, they examined their own personal abilities and responsibilities to make a difference.

Both Peterson's and Schultz's approach to a "thinking curriculum" (as well as the approaches taken by many of the community-engaged programs described earlier in this chapter) share several characteristics. First, teachers encourage students to ask questions rather than absorb pat answers—to think about their attachments and commitments to their local, national, and global communities. Second, teachers provide students with the information (including competing narratives) they need to think about subject matter in substantive ways. In other words, they employ multiple perspectives in the service of critical analysis. Third, they eschew the kind of memorization and regurgitation that teaches only one interpretation of historical and contemporary events. Fourth, they root instruction in local contexts, working within their own specific surroundings and circumstances because it is not possible to teach democratic forms of thinking without providing an environment to think about. This last point makes nationally standardized tests difficult to reconcile with in-depth critical thinking about issues that matter. Finally, many of these goals can be accomplished by engaging students in community projects that offer students opportunities to engage as personally responsible, participatory, and social justice–oriented citizens. This short set of guidelines is summarized in Figure 8.1.

Figure 8.1. Teachers' Guide to a Thinking, Engaged Curriculum

- Encourage students to ask questions rather than absorb pat answers—to think about their attachments and commitments to their local, national, and global communities.
- Provide students with the information (including competing narratives) they need to think about subject matter in substantive ways.
- Avoid the kind of memorization and regurgitation that teaches only one interpretation of historical and contemporary events.
- Root instruction in local contexts, working within your own specific surroundings and circumstances because it is not possible to teach democratic forms of thinking without providing an environment to think about.
- Engage students in community projects that encourage personal responsibility, participation, and critical analysis.

I have also included in Figure 8.2 a list of suggestions that parents can use at home with children—a few guidelines for a "thinking curriculum" that parents may find useful.

Figure 8.2. A Thinking Curriculum: Five Things Parents Can Do With Their Students to Encourage Critical Thinking

Although this book focuses on schools, some parents might be interested in what they can do at home to foster critical thinking. Here are five simple approaches:

1. Watch the news together, or read a newspaper together. Encourage questions about events in the community and the world. Do a search on the Web together for three different perspectives on the same issue you just read or heard about.

2. Read a section of a school textbook with your child. Ask him or her who might have written the section (the idea that a person or group of people actually wrote a textbook reminds us that the words are not sacrosanct but rather represent the views of a particular time and place). Ask your child to think about whether a passage from a similar textbook in a different state or province or country would tell the story the same way. Why? Why not?

3. Encourage questions, even when you don't have the answers. Don't push aside questions about homeless people a child might see on the street, or about why so-and-so has a big house, a pool, and three cars. What are all the different ways your child could imagine organizing society? What's fair? What's not? Children have a natural curiosity about fairness (who hasn't heard the phrase "it's not fair!" a million times?).

4. Talk about school itself—there's no topic more interesting and one that a child knows a bit about (from a child's perspective). Yes, your child must follow (most) school rules. But that does not mean your child shouldn't think about those rules and procedures and why things are done that way. Are the rules fair? Are they necessary? Would teachers be able to manage a classroom without rules in place? How would your child organize a classroom or a curriculum or a school? Have him or her draw a picture of the ideal school. What would it look like architecturally? How would teaching and learning be organized? What problems might be foreseen in this school? How could they be avoided?

5. For at least some questions your child asks you, respond with questions of your own: "What do you think?"; "How can we find out?"; "What would _____ (someone else who has a different interest in the issue at hand) think about this?"

Whether in the school or at home, in after-school clubs, or on a sports team, learning about one's place in the world, about how one participates in social and civic affairs, and about critical analysis of ideas is something that takes place not alone or even between two people. Civic and social goals are always learned within a community.

ENGAGING WITH THE COMMUNITY

Ask someone active in his or her community to describe a powerful experience working for change, and you will probably get a story heavily infused with a sense of camaraderie, collaboration, and connection to others doing similar work. Students also need to know that civic engagement is not an individual, private endeavor. In fact, when we say that schools should "teach every student good citizenship," we risk implying that these goals are derived exclusively from personal attributes rather than enabled and shaped through interactions and connections among individuals within a community. Psychologists, sociologists, and anthropologists have long recognized that an individual's values and commitments are not predetermined human characteristics but rather are products of family, community, and the social setting.[20] Cultivating commitments to democratic citizenship requires associating with others who recognize and reinforce the importance of these priorities.

> Despite the importance of connections to others who deem civic participation exciting and valuable, few educational programs make developing a supportive community an explicit curricular goal.

These connections are especially important in a culture that does little to reinforce the value of civic participation. Consider that for most school-age children, the number of trips to the mall is exponentially higher than those to the voting booth, to community meetings, and so on. Despite the importance of connections to others who deem civic participation exciting and valuable, few educational programs make developing a supportive community an explicit curricular goal. However, the programs I described in this chapter and many others consciously develop communities of support and foster connections with role models who are engaged in community work.

Students need to be part of social communities that have the strength to counter the prevailing cultural emphasis on individualism and personal gain. Like sports teams and religious groups, communities of civic

Students need to be part of social communities that have the strength to counter the prevailing cultural emphasis on individualism and personal gain.

actors unite people around a common sense of purpose. Instead of winning a pennant, these communities focus on improving society. Some programs team students with accomplished civic actors; some invite role models to speak to the class. Just as it is natural to introduce aspiring students to architects or scientists or social workers, if we want students to think about the connections between their academic work and their communities, then meeting people who exemplify those connections can be powerful. Many programs use connections to the past to show students the possibilities for the future—that ordinary people can work together to improve society and achieve extraordinary results.

CHAPTER 9

Seven Myths About Education

When it comes to a thinking curriculum and community involvement, a number of stubborn myths have continually derailed the best of intentions. Some of these myths are rooted in a view of education that differs from the one promoted in this book. Others are more like misunderstandings. Both kinds hinder the development and adoption of the kinds of school activities that foster thinking, engaged citizens.

MYTH 1: NATIONAL STANDARDS ENSURE QUALITY EDUCATION

The relatively uncritical and universal acceptance among school reformers of the importance of so-called standards, rubrics, and uniform assessment tools for teaching and learning is at once predictable and misguided. It is predictable because the idea that we should clearly articulate educational goals and then devise methods for determining whether those goals are met is irresistibly tidy. After all, how can teachers pursue high-quality lessons if they do not know what they are trying to teach and whether students are learning? Uncritical acceptance of even such a common-sense–seeming idea, however, is misguided for the following reason: Education is first and foremost about human relationship and interaction, and as anyone who tried to create a rubric for family fealty, love, or trust would discover, any effort to quantify complex human interactions quickly devolves into a fool's errand.

This does not mean that there is no place for evaluative rubrics in education, or for standards, testing, and common curriculum frameworks. A number of thoughtful education writers make the need for thoughtful measures and learning frameworks clear.[1] Moreover, I have rarely met a teacher who did not have standards; most have their own forms of rubrics or evaluative frameworks as well. But No Child Left Behind and Race to the Top legislation and related reforms that call for ever more standardized rubrics and frameworks have severely restricted teachers' abilities to act in a professional capacity and exercise professional judgment on behalf of their students. These restrictions too often result in the loss of opportunities for rich and engaging curriculum based in the experiences of teacher and students alike.

The arguably more hopeful approach represented by the newer Common Core State Standards similarly aims to provide "a consistent, clear understanding of what students are expected to learn, so teachers and parents know what they need to do to help them."[2] But despite any improvements the Common Core may have made in defining useful content, the degree to which the standards end up supporting the idea that teachers can't be trusted makes them difficult for any classroom practitioner to embrace. In the end, even "better" standards succumb to the misguided assumption that the messy human relationships at the core of all teaching and learning can and should be made uniform—the same for all students in all classrooms in all schools, regardless of local context. The best teaching and learning is never homogeneous.

MYTH 2: DISSENT SHOULD BE MEDICATED

The emphasis on so-called standards has also led to an unprecedented level of regimentation in classroom

> A quiet classroom is not necessarily a thinking classroom.

practice, which has too often resulted in school professionals mistaking predictability and order for learning. A quiet classroom is not necessarily a thinking classroom. Overprescription of drugs like Ritalin (methylphenidate) to control behaviors associated with attention deficit hyperactivity disorder (ADHD) is well-documented. But far less critical analysis has been directed at the increasing diagnosis rate for a relatively new category of illness known as conduct disorders. The more the curriculum is narrowed to focus on a highly discrete set of skills only, the greater the number of students who seem unable to control their wandering attention and control. The *Diagnostic and Statistical Manual of Mental Disorders* (DSM-V) includes a newly popular psychiatric disorder called Oppositional Defiant Disorder (ODD), defining it as "a pattern of negativistic, hostile and defiant behavior." A child with ODD, according to the DSM "often argues with adults," "actively defies or refuses to comply with adult requests or rules," and is "touchy or easily annoyed by others."[3] Various treatments and psychiatric interventions are recommended for treating ODD, including cognitive behavioral therapy and the prescription of powerful antipsychotic medications such as Risperdal (risperidone) or Zyprexa (olanzapine).

I am not a medical expert, and I do not in any way intend to disparage the difficulties children and parents might face when a child is legitimately diagnosed with ODD. It certainly is possible that there are children who have oppositional difficulties and are in need of treatment. A growing body of evidence, however, indicates that, during the same time period that school reform has continually narrowed the curriculum and increased a focus on testing and standardization, diagnoses for ODD and other childhood behavioral disorders have increased significantly and that these increases are largely attributable to concerns about student behavior in school.

In 1996, the diagnosis rate for ODD in school-age children was between 1% and 3%. By 2008, the National Institutes for Health estimated diagnosis rates between 10% and 15% for school-age children. Prevalence of ODD in primary-care settings (children ages 2–5) ranges between 4% and 17%.[4] Furthermore, as University of Chicago professor Benjamin Lahey and colleagues point out, both Oppositional Defiant Disorder and Conduct Disorder are more prevalent among youths from families of low socioeconomic status.[5] One 2012 study of admissions to a psychiatric hospital in Fort Bragg, North Carolina, found that 32.4% of admitted children were diagnosed with ODD, more than any other disorder.

The implications of the rise in ODD diagnoses among school-age children led Oregon educator Norm Diamond to suggest that a new as-of-yet undiagnosed disease was sweeping the nation. He coined this new disease CAD: Compliance Acquiescent Disorder. Symptoms for CAD, Diamond joked, can be seen when a student often "defers to authority," "reflexively obeys rules," "believes the commercial media," "fails to argue back," and "stays restrained when outrage is warranted."[6] Like Diamond, I wonder if we had an inventory for CAD, whether we might find a virtual epidemic of the disease. As the technocratization and dehumanization of the curriculum continues, we are increasingly at risk of fostering an entire generation of those who—as education critic Alfie Kohn put it—have lost the capacity to be outraged by outrageous things.[7] Indeed, at the same time that schools eliminate opportunities for in-depth connections between the subject matter that students study and the sociopolitical world beyond the classroom, thousands of children who show resistant behavior, perhaps refusing to "comply with adult requests or rules" are being classified as mentally ill, disciplined, counseled, and in some cases, medicated.

MYTH 3: THE ONLY WAY TO TEACH DEMOCRATIC THINKING IS TO MAKE THE ENTIRE SCHOOL DEMOCRATIC

There are plenty of educators who agree that a thinking curriculum is important and that critique and dissent are useful skills for democratic citizenship. But even if educators can agree that schools have an important role to play in educating democratic citizens, they can't seem to agree on what that might mean for teachers and students in classrooms and schools. Some believe that the best way to teach democracy is through rigorous study of the workings of government, the history of democratic institutions, and the hard-won struggles in which democratic societies have engaged in order to preserve and strengthen democracy. Others hope teachers and students will take education outside the classroom into the community so that academic goals can be better matched to social and community projects. Still others want schools themselves to become more democratic; these advocates point to the presumed hypocrisy of teaching about democracy in a profoundly nondemocratic institution like the traditional school.

Which is the best method? As in so many questions in education, there is no one-size-fits-all answer. Much depends on the specific goals implied by "educating for democracy." As discussed in the previous chapters, democracy means different things to different people, and among educators and school reformers, the aspects of democracy that are seen as most important and the best methods for furthering these goals both vary a great deal. Still, one of the enduring and frustrating myths about democratically oriented teaching and learning is that the only way to teach democracy is to model it fully in the classroom and the school.

Few educators would argue with the idea that context matters. It is not just the content of what we teach that is important, but also how we teach and the condition of

> Even if educators can agree that schools have an important role to play in educating democratic citizens, they can't seem to agree on what that might mean for teachers and students in classrooms and schools.

the surrounding environment in which we teach. Indeed, what is modeled for students might be more important than the books they read or the class lessons in which they engage. Nowhere might this be more visible than in the appalling conflict between what teachers are supposed to teach regarding democratic participation and the non-democratic nature of teachers' workplaces. Most teachers are hardly democratic citizens of their own schools. "Do as I say and not as I do" seems a naively hopeful reflection of the way in which many teachers and students experience lessons about democracy in schools.

Yet many (self-proclaimed) progressive educators insist that only by modeling democracy in the classroom and school can we teach any valuable lessons about what it means to be a good democratic citizen. I am more convinced than ever that the kind of teaching for democracy pursued in schools varies at least as much as the different visions of the good citizen discussed earlier. There is no one pedagogy matched inextricably to certain kinds of educational outcomes.

Interestingly, those educators who might place their goals for democratic education most squarely in the social justice camp are also those who often make the case that social justice can only be taught through the kind of "progressive" pedagogy that engages the students in every aspect of the curriculum—deciding what should be taught, choosing the focus of inquiry, researching the issues, and presenting to peers what they have found. Yet how many of those school reformers and practitioners first recognized the need for political engagement by sitting through a university lecture by a dynamic professor who changed the way they thought about history, politics, and social justice? Berkeley education professor Daniel Perlstein wrote a superb study of the Mississippi Freedom Schools of the 1960s showing, in part, that although their message was always deeply democratic and oriented toward social justice, their pedagogy was not.[8] Indeed, Lisa Delpit, in "The Silenced Dialogue: Power and Pedagogy in Educating Other People's Children," argued persuasively that some Black parents and teachers view progressive pedagogy as a concerted effort to keep less-advantaged students from learning the "culture of power" that progressive change toward justice demands.[9] In her eyes, some parents of African American children would prefer that their children be told exactly what to do, how to spell correctly, the rules of grammar, and so on, because these rules and codes of the culture of power are exactly what their children need to know to get ahead. "If you are not already a participant in the culture of power," Delpit writes, "being told explicitly the rules of that culture makes acquiring power easier."[10] So—gasp!—direct instruction, when used in this way, might be a means toward an indisputably democratic goal.

The absence of a monolithic relationship between particular teaching strategies and related educational goals works the other way as well. There have been many successful efforts throughout history in teaching profoundly nondemocratic lessons through what appeared to be democratic means. Most of us associate fascism with goose-stepping soldiers marching on order from above. But one need only examine the methods of the Hitler Youth brigades to note how "progressive" were aspects of their pedagogy—inclusive (within their own group, at least), community oriented, highly social, collective, and cooperative.[11] The medium, it would seem, does not always make the message.

One of the fathers of progressive education himself—John Dewey—broke ranks with the Progressive Education Association that he had founded because of the dogmatic homage to "child-centered" pedagogy that began to grip the organization. In *Experience and Education*, he wrote passionately that "an educational philosophy which professes to be based on the idea of freedom may become as dogmatic as ever was the traditional education which is reacted against."[12]

To be sure, teaching for democratic understanding requires attention to the democratic (or nondemocratic nature) of the classroom and the school in which the teaching occurs. But it is clear from examining the myriad of excellent programs that abound that educators need not limit themselves to one particular strategy in order to achieve democratic learning goals. Rather, those educators who are interested in critical thinking and other democratic goals might do better to examine the underlying beliefs and ideological assumptions conveyed by the content of their curriculum. Teaching for democracy and teaching democratically are not always the same. To the extent that an overemphasis on pedagogy detracts from a clear examination of the underlying content and values of the lesson, the conflation of pedagogy and content might serve to conserve rather than transform educational goals.

MYTH 4: WHEN IT COMES TO COMMUNITY-BASED EXPERIENCES, KNOWLEDGE MUST ALWAYS PRECEDE ACTION (YOU HAVE TO KNOW STUFF BEFORE YOU DO STUFF)

On the other side of the ideological spectrum lies those who are convinced that facts are the holy grail of education in democratic societies, or for that matter, in any society. Witness the current obsession with standardized tests that seek to find out all the pieces of information tidbits that students don't know and punish teachers, principals, and the students themselves accordingly. The calls for "back-to-basics" education and the late-night television comedy shows that seek out citizens who can be caught not knowing answers to "basic" questions are symptoms of this counter-educational trend.

Certain policymakers and politicians mistake the logic of what needs to be taught with the logic of how one learns. In *The Child and the Curriculum*, John Dewey distinguished the "logical" from the "psychological." By logical, he meant the sensible ordering of the curriculum into steps and categories to make it possible to undertake the enterprise of teaching. But the "psychological" represents the child—how the child learns, what interests and experiences the child brings to the learning encounter. To teach means to move back and forth between these two reflections of the educational context, to guide the learning according to adult notions of what needs to be taught, all the while maintaining a keen focus on the interests, experiences, and ambitions of each individual child.[13] Educators must not confuse the logic of what they teach with how they teach.

The implications for a thinking curriculum can be seen in the tensions that arise when teachers seek to teach about democratic participation within school and classroom settings that are myopically focused on the narrowest possible conception of "knowledge." Not only do students tend to learn more "facts" through authentic participation in meaningful projects of concern, but engagement in such projects of democratic importance is rarely driven by the acquisition of facts only. In short, knowledge does not necessarily lead to participation. In many programs we studied that emphasized teaching about the workings of democratic government, legislative procedures, elections, and so on, students gained solid factual knowledge without necessarily gaining the inclination or the conviction required to participate. In fact, we found that often it worked the other way around: Participation led to the quest for knowledge. Once students gained experiences in the community, they tended to ask deep and substantive questions that led them to research information they knew little about and, until then, had little inclination to learn.

Furthermore, the hidden curriculum of fact-focused classrooms too often emphasizes pleasing authority rather than developing convictions. In these classrooms and schools, it would be difficult for students to stand up for what they believe through authentic participation in community affairs. Current classroom discourse too often reduces teaching and learning to exactly the kind of mindless fact-absorption and rule-following that makes students unable to make principled stands and participate democratically in social and political affairs. Conversely, students who acquire knowledge in conjunction with community experiences gain an understanding of knowledge as fluid, collaborative, and context-driven.

MYTH 5: TEACHERS WHO CARE ABOUT WHETHER STUDENTS CAN THINK FOR THEMSELVES DON'T CARE ABOUT FACTS OR BASIC SKILLS

This entrenched myth is related to the one above. Educators who seek to teach students to think and to interpret information—skills and habits that are essential for citizens of any democratic nation—are often criticized for having no respect for facts. They are soft, feel-good pedagogues, this kind of critique maintains, who are more interested in process than in knowing the right answers to questions. These tendencies are vilified as unfit for a rigorous standards-based education. Somehow critics have become convinced that those who say they want students to think for themselves simply do not care whether students can read, write, or perform addition or subtraction. This is plainly nonsense. We all want students to learn to read and write. Nobody wants students to be numerically illiterate. When I speak to groups of educators, policymakers, politicians, or advocacy groups, I sometimes ask whether anyone present has been recruited to join the group called "Teachers Against Kids Learning How to Add" or "School Principals in Support of Illiteracy." You should not be surprised that I have not once found anyone who is aware of these or any similar groups. What I have found is countless educators and parents who want children to know *more than* formulas. They want the knowledge that students acquire to be embedded in the service of something bigger. They want their students to develop the kinds of relationships, attitudes, dispositions, and skills that are necessary for them to engage in democratic and community life.

Teaching students to think beyond the isolated facts and skills of the fragmented curriculum will require reclaiming common assumptions about what thinking requires. There are few educators who believe

> At a time when vast databases of information are at our fingertips in seconds, facts alone represent a profoundly impoverished goal for educational achievement. Students need basic skills. But they need to be taught those skills in contexts that matter.

that facts are unimportant components of a proper education. But at a time when vast databases of information are at our fingertips in seconds, facts alone represent a profoundly impoverished goal for educational achievement. Students need basic skills. But they need to be taught those skills in contexts that matter.

MYTH 6: POLITICS SHOULD BE KEPT OUT OF SCHOOLS

"Don't be political." Being political has become an insult, as if "politics" were a four-letter word. If someone is accused of being political, it's like saying that he or she is a mud-slinging candidate running for political office for self-aggrandizement. Similarly, we often hear that schools should be "above politics" or that we should keep politics out of school. Although there is no shortage of examples of dirty politics, casting all politics in such a light denies the more noble origins of the concept. Politics is the way in which people with different values from a variety of backgrounds and interests can come together to negotiate their differences and clarify places where values conflict. Politics is, as Bernard Crick observed in his classic work *In Defence of Politics,* "a great and civilizing activity."[14] To accept the importance of politics is to strive for deliberation and a plurality of views rather than a unified perspective. If we are to educate thoughtful, civically engaged students, we must reclaim the important place for politics in classrooms and schools. Being political means embracing the kind of controversy and ideological sparring that is the engine of progress in a democracy and that gives education social meaning. The idea that "bringing politics into it" (now said disdainfully) is a pedagogically questionable act is, perhaps, the biggest threat to engaging students in thoughtful discussion.

MYTH 7: COMMUNITY-BASED
EXPERIENCES MUST BE SUCCESSFUL

When it comes to learning about citizenship and community work, success is not as straightforward as it may seem. Many schools want to ensure that students feel a sense of accomplishment from some service they've done and therefore choose simple, doable projects such as picking up litter from a nearby park. While efficacious experiences intended to promote students' sense that they are competent can support the development of stronger commitments, research indicates that opportunities for students to learn about and experience the barriers and constraints they and other civic actors frequently face can also be important.[15] First, exposure to certain kinds of constraints, although frustrating, can help students learn about the ways in which power structures, interest group influences, and technical challenges can hamper efforts toward political action and change. Second, eliminating all the frustrating obstacles that community work can entail can end up teaching students that direct service—such as individual acts of kindness and charity—is the only way to offer redress for complex social problems.

Recall the Bayside Students for Justice Program, where students engaged high-stakes problems that were difficult to solve. While other school-based programs might have students collect clothing or food for a local charity, the Bayside students were engaged in civically ambitious projects that sought to expose structural problems, sometimes foregoing more typical and bounded projects that do less to challenge existing power structures. One group investigated the lack of access to adequate health care for women and sought to get the city Board of Supervisors to allocate funds to erect a new women's health center in an underserved area. Other groups investigated complex issues such as child labor practices, bias in standardized testing, and welfare reform.

Naturally, these projects were more likely to meet with opposition than less-ambitious projects. The students were frequently turned away, ignored or, in the students' words, "not taken seriously." They didn't always gain a feeling of success in the way that students cleaning up a park might. At the same time, many of the more challenging experiences spark valuable insights. Students gain understandings of power relations and obstacles to change.

Since educators often make the choice to aim exclusively for community engagement that is likely to succeed, they too often obscure the importance of politics, social critique, and collective pursuit of systemic change. A majority of school-based, community-action programs focus on direct service activities such as tutoring, serving food, clothes collections, and blood drives, while a much smaller number concern students with politically engaged activities like drafting legislation or influencing policy—efforts that may be less likely to meet with certain success but that expose students to important social policy debates and concerns.

Tobi Walker, of the Rutgers University's Eagleton Institute of Politics, labels this phenomenon a "service/politics split." She observes that most of the students with whom she has worked on community engagement projects are "filled with disgust, disillusionment, and even dread toward politics." They want to "get things done" and "see results," but they rarely see it worthwhile to challenge institutions in power. They are eager to feed the hungry but not to think about the causes of hunger or poverty; they tutor inner-city children, but do not ask why the schools have little in the way of resources. She concludes that her students learned a great deal about how to serve but little about effecting political change.[16]

Strategies exist to promote a sense of success without obscuring the need for deeper analysis of root causes. One program in a Washington, DC, Catholic school had students work in soup kitchens but coupled their experiences with classroom work that analyzed economic, social, and political issues related to poverty and homelessness. Another program exposes students to longtime community activists who recognize small successes as parts of much larger long-term goals. Neither program provides students with complete success, but rather with a vision of a goal for which they and others could collectively strive.

> When it comes to lessons in civic engagement, it's good to succeed sometimes. But success isn't everything.

Programs that effectively leverage enthusiasm by allowing students to feel successful are valuable, to be sure, but they can also minimize the importance of examining social institutions and structures. When it comes to lessons in civic engagement, it's good to succeed sometimes. But success isn't everything.

* * *

Joseph Campbell famously expounded on the role of myths in creating a sense of awe, wonder, and gratitude.[17] Myths have the power to uplift and provoke thinking about possibilities that are not yet realized. The myths I describe here, however, have the opposite effect. In fact, our culture is now suffused with so many damaging myths about schools and classroom practice that many of the worst ideas for education reform have grown out of the false beliefs these myths keep alive. It is a truism that myths are based not on evidence but on unproven beliefs. That's why efforts to demonize teachers, privatize schools, and create an ever more restrictive curriculum thrive—not on evidence but on myths.

Yet the teachers who run the programs that were detailed in Chapter 8 demonstrate the power of evidence to lay damaging myths to rest. I have spent time with countless teachers who, in fact, have filled me with awe and a sense of what is possible in our schools. There are a myriad of ways to teach the skills of democratic thinking and engagement. All students do not need to learn the same inflexible common core of material in order to have a nation of well-educated citizens. Students do not need to be sedated to learn. Schools do not need to avoid controversy and politics, and they can teach students to participate in civic and community life in creative and provocative ways. What we need are strong public commitments to support the kinds of schools that strengthen democratic life and that educate our children for the common good.

CHAPTER 10

What Kind of School?

In a memorable scene from the classic movie *Ferris Bueller's Day Off,*
the teacher, played by Ben Stein, is lecturing to students about the
Great Depression, droning on and on about the Hawley-Smoot Tariff
Act and voodoo economics. The students stare ahead in disbelief,
boredom, and fatigue (with at least one asleep at his desk, drooling).
"In 1930," the teacher says in monotone, "the Republican-controlled
House of Representatives, in an effort to alleviate the effects of the
. . . Anyone? Anyone? . . . the Great Depression, passed the . . .
Anyone? Anyone? The tariff bill."[1] It's both painful and funny to
watch because we have all been in similar classes—economics, civics,
or history classes where teaching and learning has been reduced to
an anesthetizing hum of contextless facts and dates. What year did
the Norman Invasion begin? How many members comprise the U.S.
House of Representatives? Who signs bills to become laws? Anyone?
Anyone? Science, mathematics, and English, too, can easily be reduced to mind-numbing drivel when subject matter is sliced and diced
into discreet bits of information and routines without a unifying sense
of meaning or relevance.

Teaching and learning does not have to be that way. You may have
examples from your own schooling when the material you were learning became deeply connected to important issues and themes, where
learning was not about memorization and recitation, but about thinking and acting. You may have had a
particularly talented and passionate
teacher or the curricular materials
you were using may have suggested
thought-provoking, real-world connections or both. Every *Ferris Bueller*
type moment can be countered with
teachers—both on-screen and off—
who, in their classroom practice, see

> The problem is not that we do
> not know how to make school
> meaningful and engaging, but
> rather that the goal has too
> often been buried under our
> obsession with standardization,
> test preparation, and facts and
> information.

endless possibility and imagination. The problem is not that we do not know how to make school meaningful and engaging, but rather that the goal of making schools meaningful, engaging, and thoughtful has too often been buried under our obsession with standardization, test preparation, and facts and information.

This renewed concern with teaching facts and information is especially curious in an age when facts about anything and everything are available at our fingertips in a matter of seconds. Near ubiquitous access to Web searches means that the acquisition of knowledge should no longer be the emphasis of schooling. Thinking about how we employ knowledge in the service of cognitive, social, moral, political, and economic goals, however, has never been more important. It's that kind of learning that children—especially those growing up in democratic societies where they will be asked to participate in decisions that affect all of us—need more than anything else. Programs and activities that teach students how to think deserve far more attention in our classrooms.

All schools teach citizenship. The concern of this book has been to ask, *What kind of citizenship*? What political and ideological interests are embedded in varied conceptions of citizenship? What kind of citizens are the schools trying to shape? Varied priorities—personal responsibility, participatory citizenship, and justice-oriented citizenship—embody significantly different beliefs regarding the capacities and commitments citizens need in order for democracy to flourish; and they carry significantly different implications for pedagogy, curriculum, evaluation, and educational policy.

First, school programs that hope to develop personally responsible citizens may not be effective at increasing participation in local and national civic affairs. In fact, efforts to pursue some conceptions of personal responsibility can undermine efforts to prepare participatory and justice-oriented citizens.

Second, the study of the Madison County Youth Service League and of Bayside Students for Justice that I described in Chapter 7 demonstrates the importance of distinguishing between programs that emphasize participatory citizenship and those that emphasize the pursuit of justice. While each program was effective in achieving its goals, qualitative and quantitative data regarding these programs demonstrated important differences in each program's impact. Programs that champion participation do not necessarily develop students' abilities to analyze and critique root causes of social problems and vice versa.

Although many who are committed to the democratic purposes of education may extol the value of linking priorities related to participation, the evidence from practice indicates that this outcome is not guaranteed. If both goals are priorities, those designing and implementing curriculum must give both explicit attention.

From the standpoint of research and evaluation, the implications for those who are interested in the development of democratic values and capacities are significant. Studies that fail to reflect the varied range of educational priorities in relation to democratic values and capacities will tell only part of the story. Moreover, because the desirability of many politically relevant outcomes is tightly tied to one's political preferences, consensus among scholars regarding "right" answers or sometimes even "better" answers to many relevant questions may be hard to achieve. Knowing, for example, whether a student, after experiencing a particular program, now places greater emphasis on recycling or on environmental regulation does not enable us to say that a program was effective. However, it does help us understand the program's effects.

Over the years that I have been conducting this kind of research with Joe Kahne and other colleagues, we have emphasized the differences between programs rather than suggesting that one is better than another. But we have never meant to imply a sense of neutrality with respect to varied conceptions of democratic values. Instead, we mean to emphasize that the choices we make are political choices and that the interests of varied groups are often deeply embedded in the ways that we think about and study efforts to educate for democracy. For example, we can focus on whether a given curriculum changes students' sense of personal responsibility, government responsibility, or employer responsibility. If we ask only about personal responsibility (and if discussions of personal responsibility are disconnected from analysis of the social, economic, and political context), we may well be reinforcing a highly individualistic and often status-quo notion of citizenship. Yet this is the focus of many programs and of their associated evaluations. If citizenship also requires collective participation and critical analysis of social structures, then other lenses are needed as well.

Clearly, highlighting the political significance of different curricular choices must be done with care. Such dialogues may help clarify what is at stake, but raising these issues can also lead to dysfunctional stalemates and deepen differences rather than prompt more thoughtful inquiry. Yet not all discord is bad—when the stakes are high, conflict may be both likely and appropriate. Those of us who design and teach these curricula and those studying its impact must be aware of different—and at times conflicting—visions of citizenship and their implications. Democracy is not self-winding. Students need to be taught to participate in our democracy, and different programs aim at different goals. The choices we make have consequences for the kind of society we ultimately help to create.

What kind of society are we hoping our schools and their teachers will help to bring about? Teaching and learning in democratic societies has special requirements. Chief among these are that students know how to think critically, ask questions, evaluate policy, and work with others toward change that moves democracy forward. Educating future citizens for democratic societies requires that schools:

> Teaching and learning in democratic societies has special requirements. Chief among these are that students know how to think critically, ask questions, evaluate policy, and work with others toward change that moves democracy forward.

- Teach students how to ask questions
- Expose students to multiple perspectives and viewpoints on important issues that affect everyone's lives
- Provide opportunities to analyze and discuss different viewpoints
- Show that "facts" are less stable than is often thought
- Engage controversial issues

In Chapter 4, I pointed out that in the same way that Darwin's theory of natural selection depends on genetic variation, any theory of democracy depends on multiple perspectives and ideas. Darwin saw the need for spontaneous variations in the natural world as necessary for evolutionary progress of the species. Those of us who see in schools the possibility for social change and improvement should similarly embrace a multiplicity of ideas in the school curriculum. Students should be exposed to multiple perspectives and taught to think and to dialogue in the kinds of expansive ways on which democracy thrives.

Yet there are a number of forces that steadily work against these goals. Considerable effort has been devoted to making schools over in the image of job-training institutions, concerned only with individual achievement in a narrow range of subjects. The move toward purely individualistic and instrumental goals has also ushered in an obsession with standardization and sameness, orderliness over free inquiry. And that, in turn, has created a strange focus on particular bodies of knowledge and "facts" to the exclusion of other perspectives and interpretations. In too many classrooms, students are told what to think rather than how to think.

Today, we trust teachers less and less and standardized tests more and more. We prescribe medications to a shockingly high percentage of students to make them attentive and "normal" (even when a *majority* of children in some neighborhood schools are deemed "not normal"—can a majority of children really be "not normal"?). Reform policies at the highest levels are made without any evidence that they will work. And students are treated alternately as blank slates waiting to be trained, as clients waiting to be served, or as consumers waiting to buy. In some schools, the entire school day is reduced to almost nothing but test preparation in only two subject areas: math and literacy. Meanwhile elaborate reward and punishment systems are instituted to keep students engaged, and teachers are all but ignored in the reform deliberations that create this mess. It sometimes seems that in the quest to improve students' focus and interest, the only thing we are not trying is to actually make the curriculum interesting and worth focusing on. Anyone? Anyone?

In the face of these conditions, it would seem easy to lose hope. But that would be shortsighted. Across North America and elsewhere in the world, parents, teachers, administrators, and students are increasingly convinced that we need curriculum worth focusing on and schools that make that possible. They are increasingly impatient with calls for educational standards, accountability measures, and assessment tools that consistently fail to capture a broad variety of classroom goals, including civic engagement, participation, and the kinds of thinking skills that effective democratic citizenship requires. The "Opt-Out" movement (in which parents opt their children out of standardized assessments) has reached a fever pitch in many jurisdictions. In spring 2014, more than 70% of parents in three Brooklyn schools refused to allow their children to take state standardized tests because of their concern over the impoverished test-prep curriculum the tests bring about. Teachers at Garfield High School in Seattle, Washington, made national headlines when they won their campaign to reject standardized tests in reading and math altogether. Pushback in almost every major North American city from Chicago to New York, Toronto to Vancouver, San Francisco to Washington, DC, Tampa to Denver are sending the message that teaching is about more than test preparation in only two subject areas. The kinds of schools we need and want are possible.

There will always be pockets of success: individual teachers, programs, schools, and even entire districts that embrace meaningful teaching and learning, that see membership in a community of citizens as an important educational goal. The end goal is for all schools to look that way. That goal may take a while.

> There will always be pockets of success: individual teachers, programs, schools, and districts that embrace meaningful teaching and learning, that see membership in a community of citizens as an important educational goal. That goal may take a while.

The late playwright and statesman Vaclav Havel observed that hope is not the same as choosing struggles that are headed for quick success: "Hope . . . is not the conviction that something will turn out well, but the certainty that something makes sense, regardless of how it turns out."[2] Hope requires, as the late Historian Howard Zinn eloquently wrote, the ability "to hold out, even in times of pessimism, the possibility of surprise."[3] The singer-songwriter-activist Holly Near expressed this artfully in her anthem to the many social change movements that have existed for as long as there have been things to improve. Change does not always happen at broadband speeds, but knowing one is part of a timeless march toward good goals makes much of what we do worthwhile. In her song "The Great Peace March," Near sings: "Believe it or not / as daring as it may seem / it is not an empty dream / to walk in a powerful path / neither the first nor the last."[4] If I could hope for one certainty in anyone's arc as a teacher and a scholar, it would be this: the knowledge that—whether in the face of successes or setbacks—we are walking in a powerful and worthwhile path.

Acknowledgments

One of the themes of this book is the collective nature of democratic citizenship. As any writer knows, producing a manuscript is also a collective undertaking. Yes, writing can be lonely, solitary work. But the full project of researching and producing a book such as this one requires the assistance and support of many.

My greatest debt goes to Joe Kahne. Joe combines complex understandings of the challenges of research with a heart-felt commitment to improving the lives of youth and young adults in a way that is rare, making him a model of an engaged scholar. He is also a dear friend. When we wrote the original article "What kind of citizen? The politics of educating for democracy" for the *American Educational Research Journal*, we did not know the degree to which researchers, school leaders, and teachers would connect with its themes (Chapters 5, 6, and 7 draw heavily from this joint written work). Since then, that article has been adapted, reprinted, and translated into a dozen other languages, allowing a broad variety of educators to help us refine the ideas (and we both are very grateful to all those who have engaged with us around those themes). The rewards from that project, however, started early on. Joe and I designed the study together, perused data together, collaborated in conversation and text, in front of computers and over plates of food, walking in cities and sitting by lakes. It is often said that two minds are better than one, and our work together is the clearest example I have of the truth behind the cliché. Our many projects together have been a testament of the power of collaborative work.

More recently, I have benefited enormously from a new collaborative endeavor with John Rogers. John is an exceptional scholar and community advocate and knows more about John Dewey's thinking and writing than anyone I know. While writing this book, we have been engaged in a project investigating what North American high schools teach about economic inequality. Although John and I have known each other for a long time, our close and constant contact through this project meant that he was always available as an enthusiastic sounding board when I needed help. He was also tremendously patient when the work made my focus for our current project less than it should have been. I am grateful to him for picking up the slack when I faltered and for the many lively exchanges we have had about educational inequality and the role of schools in democratic societies.

In that same vein, my graduate students working on the Inequality Project, Anton Birioukov, Matt Brillinger, and Agata Soroko, have been among the most astute and enthusiastic I've had the pleasure to work with. Matt conducted much-needed 12th-hour additional research for this book, especially on El Puente Academy and the Common Core State Standards. Also, thanks to Noah Spector who assisted in research on oppositional defiant disorder.

It would not be possible to list all colleagues and friends who influenced my thinking for this book, but I am especially grateful for the support of: George Bourozikas, Eran Caspi, Mickie Caspi-Klugman, J.C. Couture, Larry Cuban, Parker Duchemin, Pam FitzGerald, Nadia Franciscono, Maxine Greene, David Holton, Hillary Kunins, Gordon Lafer, Ted Leckie, Franny Nudelman, Erika Shaker, Carol Shepard, and André and Brenda Vellino. Rachelle Abrahami and Photini Sinnis helped edit Chapters 1, 2, and 3. Michael Berkowitz helped me understand the independent school context as well as good scotch. Danny Factor faithfully listened to all of my radio broadcasts and read a lot of this writing, providing smart, outside-of-the-box thinking. Bill Ayers and Bernardine Dohrn generously provided a writing retreat, housing and nourishing me with both food and conversation when I needed it most.

At the University of Ottawa, I am lucky to have supportive and engaged colleagues who are always willing to talk through a conceptual snag or offer feedback. Among them are Sharon Cook, Doug Fleming, Ruth Kane, Lorna McLean, Nicholas Ng-A-Fook, David Pare, David Rampton, and Chris Suurtamm. Special gratitude goes to Barbara Graves, Raymond LeBlanc, and Michel Laurier, both for their support and for helping to facilitate the gift of time. I am also grateful for my colleagues at CBC, including Karla Hilton, Robyn Bresnahan, Dave Brown, Mario Carlucci, Hallie Cotnam, and Stu Mills. Their banter both on and off the air always kept me in good spirits.

This book also benefited from questions asked and comments offered at numerous speaking engagements from Calgary to Chicago, New York to Vancouver, Porto Alegre, Brazil to Utrecht in the Netherlands. In addition, the wide and varied responses to my bi-weekly education segments on CBC radio remind me of the many kinds of citizens who are out there thinking about education in inspiring ways. It's both gratifying and encouraging to know that there are so many people—in national and international audiences and in notes sent to me—who care about schools, teaching, and citizenship and who are asking variations on the same questions raised in this book.

This research could not have been conducted without generous support from funders. The Surdna Foundation, under the auspices of Robert Sherman's Democratic Values Initiative, funded the initial research for Chapters 5, 6, and 7. The Social Sciences and Humanities Research Council of Canada, the Center for Information and Research on Civic Learning and Engagement, and the University of Ottawa Research Chair program provided crucial support for further research. I am very grateful.

I owe special thanks to Carole Saltz and her amazing staff at Teachers College Press, including Christina Brianik, Monica Carrera, Brian Ellerbeck, Karl Nyberg, Laura Popovics, Libby Powell, Emily Renwick, Pete Sclafani, and Leyli Shayegan. Their assistance and guidance at every step of the process was invaluable and always above and beyond what was required. This is the second book I have worked on with Sue Liddicoat who is an editor beyond compare. The book could not have been completed without her shrewd and wise contributions to both organization and prose.

My daughter Michal Leckie, and her friends Livia Kunins-Berkowitz and Ariadne Sinnis-Bourozikas shared with me their high-school perspectives on schooling at key times. My son, Ben Westheimer, told me funny and wise stories from elementary and middle school that also informed my thinking. Both Michal and Ben also were incredibly understanding of those evenings when I would disappear into my study to work. My sister, Miriam Westheimer, and brother-in-law, Joel Einleger, were always available with open ears and outstretched arms. Robin and Rosemary Leckie have always inquired about my work and well-being in the most supportive ways.

I owe the completion of this book to Barbara Leckie. She read literally dozens of drafts of this work (maybe hundreds!), providing truly brilliant feedback and critique at every stage and supported me in more ways than I can say. With all my love and gratitude, I thank you.

Finally, to my parents, Dr. Ruth Westheimer and Manfred Westheimer, who instilled in me a love of education and taught me so much about what kind of society is possible.

—Joel Westheimer, January 15, 2015

Notes

Chapter 1

1. All names of students used in this book are pseudonyms.

2. Pope-Clark, D. (2001). *Doing school: How we are creating a generation of stressed out, materialistic, and miseducated students.* New Haven, CT: Yale University Press.

3. Quotations here are derived from journals I kept in those days.

Chapter 2

1. According to one often-cited report, many of the nations I've mentioned here are among the least democratic and "least free" in the world. See www.freedomhouse.org/report-types/freedom-world

2. See, for example:

> Berliner, D. (2011). Rational responses to high stakes testing: The case of curriculum narrowing and the harm that follows. *Cambridge Journal of Education, 41*(3), 287–302.
>
> Kohn, A. (2004). *What does it mean to be well educated?* Boston, MA: Beacon Press.
>
> Llewellyn, K., Cook, S., Westheimer, J., Molina-Giron, L., & Suurtamm, K. (2007). *The state and potential of civic learning in Canada.* Ottawa, Canada: Canadian Policy Research Network.
>
> Westheimer, J., & Kahne, J. (2003, Winter). What kind of citizen? Political choices and educational goals. *Campus Compact Reader,* 1–13.

3. Kahne, J., & Middaugh, E. (2008). *Democracy for some: The civic opportunity gap in high school* (Working Paper #59). Washington, DC: The Center for Information and Research on Civic Learning (CIRCLE).

4. Rentner, D. S., Scott, C., Kober, N., Chudowsky, N., Chudowsky, V., Joftus, S., & Zabala, D. (2006). *From the capital to the classroom: Year 4 of the No Child Left Behind Act.* Washington, DC: Center on Education Policy.

5. Common Core and the Farkas Duffett Research Group. (2012). Learning less: Public school teachers describe a narrowing curriculum. Available at commoncore.org/maps/documents/reports/cc-learning-less-mar12.pdf

6. Dillon, S. (2006, March 26). Schools cut back subjects to push reading and math. *New York Times,* p. A1.

7. Campbell, P. (2006, October 18). Ballot initiatives, democracy, and NCLB. Transform Education [blog]. Available at transformeducation.blogspot.com/2006_10_01_archive.html

8. Westheimer, J. (2008, Spring). No child left thinking: Democracy at-risk in America's schools. *Independent School Magazine, 32*–40.

9. Westheimer, J. (Ed.). (2007). *Pledging allegiance: The politics of patriotism in American schools.* New York, NY: Teachers College Press.

10. Alexander, L. (2003). Senator Alexander's American history and civics bill passes Senate unanimously. Press Release, Senator Alexander's office, June 20, 2003.

11. That bill died on the senate floor but had it passed, schools would have been required to surrender teaching materials to the state superintendent of public instruction, who then could have withheld state aid.

12. Arizona Bill: www.azleg.gov/legtext/48leg/2r/proposed/h.1108rp2.doc.htm
Texas Bill: www.tfn.org/site/DocServer/20...pdf?docID=3201
Florida Bill: www.historians.org/publications-and-directories/perspectives-on-history/september-2006/history-defined-in-florida-legislature
See also: Immerwahr, D. (2008). The fact/narrative distinction and student examinations in history. *The History Teacher, 41*(2), 199–206.

13. Dolinski, C. (2006, May 18). Whose facts? *Tampa Tribune,* p. A5.

14. Glenza, J. (2014, September 30). Colorado teachers stage mass sick-out to protest US history curriculum changes. *The Guardian.* Available at www.theguardian.com/education/2014/sep/29/colorado-teachers-us-history-sickout-protest-contracts-jefferson

15. Ibid.

16. Jacobs, P. (2014, September 26). Colorado high school students are protesting a proposed curriculum they say censors US history. *Business Insider.* Available at www.businessinsider.com/colorado-students-protest-curriculum-changes-2014-9

17. Milligan, S. (2014, October 3). A civics lesson from students: Protests in Colorado show what being a citizen is all about [blog]. Available at www.usnews.com/opinion/blogs/susan-milligan/2014/10/03/a-civics-lesson-from-jefferson-county-colorado-school-board-protests

18. BBC News. (2002). Public schools "spoon-feed" students. Available at news.bbc.co.uk/1/hi/education/1844620.stm

19. Thornton, S. (2005). Incorporating internationalism in the social studies curriculum. In N. Noddings (Ed.), *Educating citizens for global awareness* (pp. 81–92). New York, NY: Teachers College Press.

Chapter 3

1. National Council for Excellence in Education. (1983). *A nation at risk.* Washington, DC: United States Department of Education.

2. Westheimer, J. (2012). Ontario civics teachers talk about the effects of EQAO testing on classroom practice. Unpublished manuscript. Faculty of Education, University of Ottawa, Ontario, Canada.

3. Sahlberg, P. (2012, June 29). How GERM is infecting schools around the world. *The Washington Post*. [blog: The Answer Sheet web log by Valerie Strauss]. Available at www.washingtonpost.com/blogs/answer-sheet/post/how-germ-is-infecting-schools-around-the-world/2012/06/29/gJQAVELZAW_blog.html

4. Ravitch, D. (2013, February 26). Why I cannot support the common core standards. [blog]. Available at dianeravitch.net/2013/02/26/why-i-cannot-support-the-common-core-standards

5. Maxine Greene credits John Dewey with reminding us that "facts are mean and repellent things until we use imagination to open intellectual possibilities." From Greene, M. (2006, Winter). Jagged landscapes to possibility. *Journal of Educational Controversy*, *1*(1), 1.

6. For a spirited discussion of this trend, see Kuhn, J. (2014). *Fear and learning in America: Bad data, good teachers, and the attack on public education*. New York, NY: Teachers College Press; see also Ravitch, D. (2013). *Reign of error: The hoax of the privatization movement and the danger to America's public schools*. New York, NY: Knopf Doubleday.

Chapter 4

1. Holt, J. (1982). *How children fail*. New York, NY: Delacorte Press, p. 155.

2. See, for example, Barbara Knighton (2003). No child left behind: The impact on social studies classrooms. *Social Education, 67*.

3. Calder's Fall 2000 speech is quoted in Relic, P. (2000, Winter). The trouble with the standards movement. *Independent School Magazine*. Available at www.nais.org/Magazines-Newsletters/ISMagazine/Pages/The-Trouble-with-the-Standards-Movement.aspx

4. Canadian Association of Principals. (2007, March 9). Valid uses of student testing as part of authentic, comprehensive student assessment—A statement of concern from Canada's school principals. Available at www.cdnprincipals.org/CAP_Position_on_Student_Testing-Version1.doc

5. See McMurrer, J. (2007). *Choices, changes, and challenges: Curriculum and instruction in the NCLB era*. Center on Education Policy. The Jack Jennings quotation is from a related policy speech, available at www.whitman.edu/rhetoric/110-pages/no-child-left-behind-sara.htm

6. Breakfast program information:

Maryland State Department of Education. Classroom breakfast scores high in Maryland. Available at www.marylandpublicschools.org/NR/rdonlyres/CA432B36-F5D2-41DA-9E0D-4D01C373AA75/1541/Classroom_Breakfast.pdf

Maryland State Department of Education. Meals for achievement. Available at www.marylandpublicschools.org/msde/programs/schoolnutrition/meals_achieve.htm

Massachusetts Department of Education. Available at www.doe.mass.edu/cnp/nprograms/sbp/

Ottawa School Breakfast Program. Available at www.
ottawaschoolbreakfastprogram.ca/faq.asp

Meyers, A., Sampson, A., Weitzman, M., Rogers, B., & Kayne, H.
(1989). School breakfast program and school performance. *American
Journal of Diseases of Children, 143,* 1234–1239. Available at www.
polemicandparadox.com/2009/06/school-breakfast-program.html

7. Hammer, K. (2011). An ancient profession adjusts to the 21st-century global classroom. *The Globe and Mail.* Available at www.theglobeandmail.com/news/
national/an-ancient-profession-adjusts-to-the-21st-century-global-classroom/
article574329/

8. Dewey, John. Plan of Organization of the University Primary School, printed as appendix in Wirth, A. (1966). *John Dewey as educator: His design for work in
education* (pp. 297–305). New York: John Wiley and Sons, p. 297.

9. Ibid.

Chapter 5

1. Westheimer, J., & Kahne, J. (2003, Winter). What kind of citizen? Political
choices and educational goals. *Campus Compact Reader,* 1–13.

2. For example, Westheimer, J. & Kahne, J. (2004). What kind of citizen? The
politics of educating for democracy. *American Educational Research Journal, 41*(2),
237–269; Kahne, J. & Westheimer, J. (2006, April). The limits of efficacy: Educating citizens for a democratic society. *PS: Political Science and Politics, 39*(2), 289–296.;
Westheimer, J., & Kahne, J. (2002). Educating for democracy. In R. Hayduk & K.
Mattson (Eds.). (2002). *Democracy's moment: Reforming the American political system
for the 21st century* (pp. 91–107). Lanham, MD: Rowman & Littlefield; Kahne, J.,
& Westheimer, J. (2003, September). Teaching democracy: What schools need to
do. *Phi Delta Kappan, 85*(1), 34–40, 57–66; Westheimer, J., Kahne, J., & Rogers, B.
(1999). Learning to lead: Building on young people's desire to "do something."
New Designs for Youth Development, 15(3), 41–46.

3. Westheimer, J., & Kahne, J. (2004). What kind of citizen? The politics of
educating for democracy. *American Educational Research Journal, 41*(2), 237–269.

4. Mann, H. (1838). *First annual report.* Boston, MA: Dutton & Wentworth. See
also: Lickona, T. (1993). The return of character education. *Educational Leadership,
51*(3), 6–11; Wynne, E. A. (1986). The great tradition in education: Transmitting
moral values. *Educational Leadership, 43*(4), 4–9.

5. Available at charactercounts.org/sixpillars.html

6. Available at pointsoflight.org

7. Newmann, F. (1975). *Education for citizen action: Challenge for secondary curriculum.* Berkeley, CA: McCutchan; also see Verba, S., Schlozman, K. L., & Brady, H.
E. (1995). *Voice and equality: Civic volunteerism in American politics.* Cambridge, MA:
Harvard University Press, for an empirical analysis of the importance of such skills
and activities. Interestingly, the importance of participation for community life
has been emphasized for a long time. In 1916, the education philosopher John

Dewey put forward a vision of "Democracy as a Way of Life" and emphasized participation in collective endeavors. To support the efficacy of these collective efforts, he also emphasized commitments to communication, experimentation, and scientifically informed dialogues. Such commitments were also prevalent in the educational writings of Thomas Jefferson and Benjamin Franklin, among others, who viewed informed participation in civic life as a fundamental support for a democratic society and saw education as a chief means for furthering this goal. See Pangle, L. S., & Pangle, T. L. (1993). *The learning of liberty.* Lawrence, KS: University Press of Kansas.

8. See, for example: Kaestle, C. F. (2000). Toward a political economy of citizenship: Historical perspectives on the purposes of common schools. In L. Mc-Donnell, P. M. Timpane, & R. Benjamin (Eds.), *Rediscovering the democratic purposes of education* (pp. 47–72). Lawrence, KS: University Press of Kansas; Smith, R. M. (1997). *Civic ideals: Conflicting visions of citizenship in U.S. history.* New Haven, CT: Yale University Press; Schudson, M. (1998). *The good citizen: A history of American civic life.* New York, NY: Free Press.

9. Rugg, H. (1966). Reconstructing the curriculum: An open letter to professor Henry Johnson commenting on committee procedure as illustrated by the report of the joint committee on history and education for citizenship. In W. Parker (Ed.), *Educating the democratic mind* (pp. 45–60). New York, NY: State University of New York Press, p. 47. (Original work published 1921)

10. See, for example: Fine, M. (1995). *Habits of mind: Struggling over values in America's classrooms.* San Francisco, CA: Jossey Bass; Kliebard, H. M. (1995). *The struggle for the American curriculum: 1893–1958.* New York, NY: Routledge.

11. Another important Social Reconstructionist was George Counts, who asked, "Dare the School Build a New Social Order?" He wanted educators to critically assess varied social and economic institutions, while also "engag[ing] in the positive task of creating a new tradition in American life" (p. 262). Counts, G. (1932). Dare progressive education be progressive? *Progressive Education, 9,* 257–263.

12. Kilpatrick, W. (1918). The project method. *Teachers College Record, 19*(4), p. 323.

13. Dewey, J. (1959). The school and society. In M. S. Dworkin (Ed.), *Dewey on education: Selections* (pp. 33–90). New York, NY: Teachers College Press. (Original work published 1900)

14. See, for example: Faunce, R. C., & Bossing, N. L. (1951). *Developing the core curriculum.* New York, NY: Prentice Hall; Alberty, H. (1953). *Reorganizing the high school curriculum.* New York, NY: MacMillan.

15. Giles, H. H., McCutchen, S. P., & Zechiel, A. N. (1942). *Adventure in American education. (Volume II). Exploring the curriculum: The work of the thirty from the viewpoint of curriculum consultants.* New York, NY: Harper & Brothers.

16. Bennett, W. J. (1985). Education for democracy. Paper presented at the regular meeting of the Consejo Interamericano para la Education, la Ciencia, y la Cultura, Washington, DC. Quoted in: Westheimer, J., & Kahne, J. (2003, Winter).

What kind of citizen? Political choices and educational goals. *Campus Compact Reader*, p. 2.

Chapter 6

1. Holt, J. (1982). *How children fail*. New York, NY: Delacorte Press, p. 234.

2. National Association of Secretaries of State. (1999). *New millennium project—Phase I: A nationwide study of 15–24-year-old youth*. Alexandria, VA: Tarrance Group.

3. See the following: Westheimer, J., & Kahne, J. (2001). Social justice, service learning, and higher education: A critical review of research. *The School Field, 12*(5/6). Adapted from Kahne, J., Westheimer, J., & Rogers, B. (2000, Fall). Service learning and citizenship: Directions for research, *Michigan Journal of Community Service Learning, 42*–51.

Chapter 7

1. Barber, B. (1984). *Strong democracy: Participatory politics for a new age*. Berkeley, CA: University of California Press.

2. Boyte, H. C. (2002, November 1). A different kind of politics: John Dewey and the meaning of citizenship in the 21st century. Dewey Lecture, University of Michigan.

3. See, for example: Hanna, P. R. (1936). *Youth serves the community*. New York, NY: D. Appleton-Century; Kilpatrick, W. (1918). The project method. *Teachers College Record, 19*(4), 319–335; Shor, I. (1992). *Empowering education: Critical teaching for social change*. Chicago, IL: University of Chicago Press; Youniss, J., McClellan, J. A., & Yates, M. (1997). What we know about engendering civic identity. *American Behavioral Scientist, 40*(5), 620–631.

4. Westheimer, J., & Kahne, J. (2004, Summer). What kind of citizen? The politics of educating for democracy. *American Educational Research Journal, 41*(2), 237–269.

5. The Democratic Values Initiative was funded by the Surdna Foundation, under the direction of Robert Sherman. This chapter is based on the findings from that study and is adapted from Westheimer, J., & Kahne, J. (2004, Summer). What kind of citizen? The politics of educating for democracy. *American Educational Research Journal, 41*(2), 237–269.

6. Ibid.; and Westheimer, J. & Kahne, J. (2004, April). Educating the "good" citizen: Political choices and pedagogical goals. *Political Science & Politics, 38*(2), 241–247.

7. For a related study, see Kahne, J., Chi, B., & Middaugh, E. (2006). Building social capital for civic and political engagement: The potential of high-school civics courses. *Canadian Journal of Education, 29*(2), 387–409.

Chapter 8

1. Kahne, J., & Westheimer, J. (2003, September). Teaching democracy: What schools need to do. *Phi Delta Kappan, 85*(1), 34–40, 57–66; Westheimer, J. (2004, April). The politics of civic education. *Political Science & Politics, 38*(2), 57–61.

Introduction to special issue; Westheimer, J., & Kahne, J. (2003, Winter). What kind of citizen? Political choices and educational goals. *Campus Compact Reader*, 1–13; Westheimer, J., & Kahne, J. (2004, Summer). What kind of citizen? The politics of educating for democracy. *American Educational Research Journal, 41*(2), 237–269.

2. The information included here about El Puente is drawn from a research study on democratic schools as well as from subsequent informal visits. See Westheimer, J. (2009). No child left thinking: Democracy at risk in American schools and what we need to do about it. In S. Shapiro (Ed.), *Education and hope in troubled times* (pp. 259–272). New York, NY: Routledge.

3. Quoted in Hevesi, D. (1994, September 18). Hasidic and Hispanic residents in Williamsburg try to forge a new unity. *The New York Times*. Available at www.nytimes.com/1994/09/18/nyregion/hasidic-and-hispanic-residents-in-williamsburg-try-to-forge-a-new-unity.html

4. El Puente Academy for Peace and Justice. Available at www.justicematters. org/programs/13/el-puente-academy-for-peace-and-justice

5. To date, El Puente Academy has advocated for and participated in the conversion of two properties into "Leadership Centers" that are used for a range of purposes, including after-school care, art and dance classes, tutoring, and drop-in meetings. For a description of one center, see elpuente.us/content/williamsburg-leadership-center

6. Gonzales, D. (1995, May 23). Alternative schools: A bridge from hope to social action. *New York Times*, p. B2; North Central Regional Educational Laboratory. (2000). *Viewpoints, volume 7: Small by design: Resizing America's high schools*. Naperville, IL: Learning Points Associates; Westheimer, J. (2005). Real world learning: El Puente Academy and educational change (Democratic Dialogue occasional paper series). Ottawa, Ontario. Available at DemocraticDialogue.com

7. Dewey, J. (1916). *Experience and education*. Carbondale, IL: University of Southern Illinois Press, p. 56.

8. See andoverinstitute.com/2014/07/14/spanish-511-connects-andover-students-lawrence-residents/

9. At the time, the course was called *La Presencia Hispana en los Estados Unidos*.

10. Westheimer, J., & Kahne, J. (2000). *The democratic values initiative, effective citizenry: Report to the Surdna Foundation Board*. More information about the contemporary Project V.O.I.C.E. can be found at archives.lib.state.ma.us/bitstream/handle/2452/114571/ocm52596669-LawrenceFamilyDevelopment.pdf?sequence=21

11. The Overground Railroad/Agora Project was a collaboration between six private colleges in Kentucky, Indiana, Minnesota, North Carolina, and Ohio, with Berea (Kentucky) College and the College of St. Catherine coordinating. For more information, see Kahne, J., & Westheimer, J. (2003, September). Teaching democracy: What schools need to do. *Phi Delta Kappan, 85*(1), 34–40, 57–66. See also acfnewsource.org.s60463.gridserver.com/democracy/overground_railroad.html; www.csmonitor.com/1998/0623/062398.feat.feat.7.html

12. See mikvachallenge.org; http://inside.augsburg.edu/publicachievement; and http://earthforceeducation.com

13. See www.crf-usa.org/cityworks/cityworks.html

14. generationcitizen.org

15. generationcitizen.org/the-classroom-experience

16. civiced.org/programs/wtp

17. civiced.org/students

18. Westheimer, J. (Ed.). (2007). *Pledging allegiance: The politics of patriotism in American schools*. New York, NY: Teachers College Press. Also see Peterson, B. (2007). La Escuela Fratney: A journey toward democracy. In M. Apple & J. Beane (Eds.), *Democratic schools: Lessons in powerful education* (pp. 30–61). Portsmouth, NH: Heinemann.

19. Schultz, B. D. (2008). *Spectacular things happen along the way: Lessons from an urban classroom*. New York, NY: Teachers College Press.

20. Berman, S. (1997). *Children's social consciousness and the development of social responsibility*. New York, NY: State University of New York Press.

Chapter 9

1. See, for example, Flynn, J., & Tenam-Zemach, M. (Eds.). (2013). *Rubric nation: A reader on the utility and impact of rubrics in education*. Charlotte, NC: Information Age Publishing.

2. Understanding the common core state standards initiative. Available at commoncore.pearsoned.com/index.cfm?locator=PS11Ue

3. American Psychiatric Association. (2000). *Diagnostic and statistical manual of mental disorders: DSM-IV-TR*. Washington, DC: Author; American Psychiatric Association. (2013). *Diagnostic and statistical manual of mental disorders: DSM-V-TR*. Washington, DC: Author.

4. Shaffer D., Fisher P., Dulcan, M. K., & Davies, M. (1996). The NIMH diagnostic interview schedule for children version 2.3 (DISC-2.3): Description, acceptability, prevalence rates, and performance in the MECA study. *Journal of the American Academy of Child and Adolescent Psychiatry, 35*, 865–877.

5. Lahey, B. B., Waldman, I. D., & McBurnett, K. (1999). The development of antisocial behavior: An integrative causal model. *Journal of Child Psychology and Psychiatry, 40*, 669–682; Loeber, R., Burke, J. D., Lahey, B. B., Winters, A., & Zera, M. (2000); Oppositional defiant and conduct disorder: A review of the past 10 years, part I. *Journal of the American Academy of Child & Adolescent Psychiatry, 39*(12), 1468–1484.

6. Diamond, N. (2003, Summer). Defiance is not a disease. *Rethinking Schools*. Available at www.rethinkingschools.org//cmshandler.asp?archive/17_04/defi174.shtml

7. Kohn, A. (2004, November). Challenging students and how to have more of them. *Phi Delta Kappan, 86*(3), 184–194.

8. Perlstein, D. (2002). Minds stayed on freedom: Politics and pedagogy in the African-American freedom struggle. *American Educational Research Journal, 39,* 249–277.

9. Delpit, L. (1995). The silenced dialogue: Power and pedagogy in educating other people's children. In *Other people's children: Cultural conflict in the classroom* (pp. 119–139). New York, NY: New Press.

10. Ibid., p. 127.

11. Sunker, H., & Otto, H. U. (Eds.). (1997). *Education and fascism. Political identity and social education in Nazi Germany.* London, United Kingdom: Taylor & Francis.

12. Dewey, J. (1916). *Experience and education.* Carbondale, IL: University of Southern Illinois Press, p. 22.

13. Dewey, J. (2010). *The child and the curriculum.* New York, NY: Cosimo. (Original work published 1902)

14. Crick, B. (2005). *In defence of politics.* London, United Kingdom: A&C Black, p. 9. (Original work published 1962)

15. Kahne, J., & Westheimer, J. (2006, April). The limits of efficacy: Educating citizens for a democratic society. *PS: Political Science and Politics, 39*(2), 289–296.

16. Walker, T. (2000). The service/politics split: Rethinking service to teach political engagement. *PS: Political Science and Politics, 33*(3), 647–649.

17. Campbell, J. (2004). *Pathways to bliss: Mythology and personal transformation.* Novato, CA: New World Library.

Chapter 10

1. Chinich, M. (Producer), & Hughes, J. (Director). (1986). *Ferris Bueller's Day Off* [Motion picture]. United States: Paramount Pictures.

2. Havel, V. (2004). An orientation of the heart. In P. Loeb (Ed.), *The impossible will take a little while: A citizen's guide to hope in a time of fear* (pp. 83–89). New York, NY: Basic Books, p. 82.

3. Zinn, H. (2010). *A people's history of the United States: 1492–present.* New York, NY: Harper & Row, p. 634. (Original work published 1980)

4. Near, H. (1990). Great peace march. On *Singer in the Storm* [CD]. Hawthorne, CA: Chameleon Music Group. Track 8. Used by permission.

Index

About the Author

Joel Westheimer is university research chair in democracy and education at the University of Ottawa. He is also the education columnist for CBC Radio's *Ottawa Morning* show. He began his career teaching in the New York City Public School system before obtaining a Ph.D. from Stanford University. Westheimer's award-winning books include *Pledging Allegiance: The Politics of Patriotism in America's Schools* (foreword by the late Howard Zinn) and *Among Schoolteachers: Community, Autonomy, and Ideology in Teachers' Work*, both from Teachers College Press. Westheimer lectures widely and frequently addresses radio and television audiences nationally and internationally. He lives with his wife and two children in Ottawa, Ontario. Visit his website at joelwestheimer.org for more information, or follow him @joelwestheimer.